It Will Live Forever

Traditional
Yosemite Indian
Acorn Preparation

Bev Ortiz
Photos by Raye Santos

Heyday Books
Berkeley, California
In association with Rick Heide
1991

ISBN: 0-930588-45-2
Library of Congress Card Catalog Number: 91-076689

Printed in the United States of America
10   9   8   7   6   5   4   3   2   1

Cover and interior design by DuFlon Design Associates,
    Berkeley, CA
Typeset in Berling by Rick Heide, Redwood City, CA

Historic photographs courtesy of the Yosemite
    Association

Published by Heyday Books
            P.O. Box 9145
            Berkeley, CA 94709

Dedication

This book is dedicated to the Yosemite Miwok/Paiute, past, present, and future, who are its foundation and inspiration, and to the elders who have been the teachers of each generation, especially Julia Parker's teachers: Lucy Telles, Yosemite Miwok/Paiute; Carrie Bethel, Mono Lake Paiute; Minnie Mike, Mono Lake Paiute; Ida Bishop, Northfork Mono; Molly Jackson, Yokayo Pomo; Mabel McKay, Cache Creek Pomo; Elsie Allen, Cloverdale Pomo; and it is dedicated to Julia herself who, because of her determination to carry on the old ways, and the generosity of her commitment to share these skills with others, has made this book possible.

Also, to Julia's firstborn, Virginia Parker (1949-1990), who helped her mother pound acorn and was learning the ways of her own Miwok/Paiute people.

The author, Bev Ortiz, is a park naturalist, freelance writer, and ethnographic consultant who lives in the San Francisco Bay Area. Her column, "Skills and Technology," appears in *News from Native California*.

The photographer, Raye Santos, works and lives in Yosemite National Park.

Acknowledgments

A book such as this evolves from the interest, treasured friendship, love, and kindnesses of many people. To Ralph Parker, whose loving support has given Julia the confidence to continue the old ways, go great and heartfelt thanks.

To Malcolm Margolin, I am ever grateful for the idea and publishing infrastructure needed to create this book. Malcolm has been there throughout with thoughtful words of encouragement, effusive energy, and vibrant editorial suggestions.

For many hours of commitment given this project, the warmest of thanks go to Raye Santos. Raye has given form to the words on these pages with her fine photographs and nurtured the project with her great enthusiasm.

Deepest gratitude goes to Craig Bates, Curator of Ethnography at Yosemite National Park, who has assisted Julia immeasurably in her work, joining her in years of learning. Craig also helped start me on a journey of learning about California Indian skills, shared his files of historic Yosemite acorn making articles, arranged for me to review the Yosemite Library's photo archives, and showed me where to find the photographs I needed. It was during a class taught by Craig in 1980 that I had my first opportunity to use baskets, mortar and pestle, and heated stones to make black oak acorns into food.

Thanks also to Yosemite Librarian Linda Eade for permission to use the library on her day off; and to Jim Snyder, who adjusted his research hours in the library on that certain Monday so I could, in turn, do the research I needed.

And to Kathleen Smith, Bodega Miwok/Dry Creek Pomo, who has sustained this project from beginning to end, goes much appreciation. The philosophies she has shared about her culture have challenged me to look deeply at all facets of California Indian acorn preparation, past and present.

Thanks also to Julia for patiently reviewing the many drafts of the manuscript with me; Craig, Malcolm, and Kathleen for reviewing the earliest draft; Dennis Dutton and Malcolm for editing subsequent drafts; Jeannine Gendar for editing the final draft and tirelessly overseeing the book's production; and Tracey Broderick whose proofing and editing skills gave the book its final polish.

At Julia's request, a portion of the proceeds from this book will be used to support *News from Native California*, a quarterly magazine published by Heyday Books that covers people, events, and concerns of California Indians.

— Bev Ortiz

Contents

Introduction

California's landscape reveals itself in contrasts. Fog-drenched coastal beaches, cliffs, and hills belie thirsty, sandy deserts not altogether distant. A grand expanse of rocky mountains rises amidst valleys small and large — each place uniquely suited to the native plants and animals it harbors, each plant and animal uniquely suited to its place.

These plants and animals live in a relationship with the earth developed over millenia upon millenia. Redwoods tower along well-watered northern coasts; cacti bulge with water hoarded from the infrequent rains of desert lands; alpine tundra vegetation flourishes in the freezing, windswept summits of the Sierra; marsh plants spread across wetlands draped in the music of shorebirds. Pines, oaks, scrub, grasses, and wildflowers — all have a place in California, as do the oldest, tallest, smallest (naturally stunted), and most massive trees in the world.

People have known this multi-faceted land for aeons. When non-Indians first invaded California in the late 1700s, hundreds of small, well-settled Indian groups had been thriving here for thousands of years. Generally, the people lived within small nations comprised of networks of villages. Each had a capital and its own economic, political, religious, and social tradition, developed over century upon century of living with the land.

In heavily-wooded northwest California, the people sometimes set out in redwood dugout boats to fish in rivers for salmon or in the ocean for marine mammals. In the eastern deserts people lived in nomadic family groups, harvesting plant foods such as pinenuts, and hunting game such as rabbits, with great skill. In the deserts along the Colorado River, squash, beans, and corn were farmed, while in Central California, acorn was a staple food, like rice, flour, and potatoes today.

According to estimates, the number of Indian people living here 250 years ago exceeded 300,000, making California the most populous of any comparably-sized area north of Mexico. About 100 different languages, some as similar as German and English, others as different as Chinese and English, were spoken. And within these languages were hundreds of dialects.

For those California Indians who used acorn, there were perhaps hundreds of variations in the general methods used to process it into food, each defined according to the tradition of a community, family, or individual. This book focuses on one way to cook acorns, that of Yosemite Miwok/Paiute elder Lucy Tom Parker Telles as handed down to Julia Parker.

I first met Julia Parker when I worked as a seasonal naturalist at Yosemite National Park in the late 1970s. However, it was not until 1982, when we spent time travelling together to study basketry with Pomo elder Mabel McKay, that we became friends. By this time I lived in Walnut Creek, a suburban community about 15 miles east of San Francisco Bay. Julia would journey from Yosemite by train and bus to Berkeley, where I would pick her up for the drive to the Novato home of Arlene Anderson, who hosted Mabel's class for several years.

Whenever I visited Yosemite after that, I stopped at the Indian Museum in Yosemite Valley to sit with Julia, who always had interesting stories to tell about the newest basket she was working on; the subtleties of yet another traditional skill she had mastered; or her most recent trip across California and beyond to demonstrate and teach the skills of the Yosemite Miwok/Paiute people.

On some of our visits I also found new opportunities to learn more about acorn making. In June of 1987 I assisted Julia with an acorn preparation demonstration in an oak-bejewelled wilderness park in Alameda County. It was not the first time I had the opportunity to prepare acorn with Julia. At other times, the setting had been Yosemite Valley or Kule Loklo in Point Reyes National Seashore.

Each opportunity found me amazed at the ease with which Julia's practiced hands cracked, winnowed, pounded, sifted, leached, then cooked the acorn. Each opportunity left me even more astounded and respectful of the levels of skill and nuance of method that go into the preparation of acorn, one of a huge variety of native plant and animal foods.

One day, as we walked through the Valley, Julia hurried to my side as a tree started to separate us. She explained that the old people taught her if two companions walked on opposite sides of a tree, their friendship would be broken. As we continued on our way, I walked with gratitude for the friend Julia has been to me and so many others.

Out of respect for Julia Parker, and out of respect for the food which comes from oak trees, a food which has been so widely written about, but so little understood, came the idea for an article in the quarterly magazine *News from Native California*. The wide interest shown in that article resulted in the publication of this book, which greatly refines and expands the original.

Unless indicated otherwise, the information contained herein came directly from Julia in conversations and interviews conducted between August 1986 and July 1991. In writing about Yosemite Miwok/Paiute acorn making, Julia and I tried to think about and ferret out every possible detail of the process. We even attempted to quantify amounts, weights and times as closely as possible. Since amounts are traditionally governed by experience — they are something an acorn maker knows, not measures — all numbers should be read merely as guidelines.

As Julia noted of our efforts at one point while looking at a nut, "Poor acorn being theorized!" Although we knew theory and quantification were necessary for the book, in some ways they also sully the way we look upon the food.

It is a wholly enjoyable experience to make acorn. The things which kept me wanting to know more and more about it were the smooth feel of the shell, the delightful, rhythmical sounds of processing, the magical, riveting sight and smell of the food boiling and bubbling away in the basket, and the satisfaction of gathering and preparing one's own food in a way that spans generations.

The process seemed straightforward at first glance, but every time I watched and listened to Julia as she did her work, every time I tried to copy her actions, and every question I asked made me realize anew that the complexities of preparation are at once overwhelming and awe-inspiring.

Even when it seemed that surely I had learned as much as could be known about acorn, I came up against that perennial and humbling lesson of knowledge: that the more you know, the more you find out how much you don't know. And right up to the very end, as the final drafts of this book were being prepared, I was still learning, as I will continue to learn long after this book is published.

I hope you, the reader, will learn and continue to learn too. For while this book is as complete and detailed as possible, the written word cannot replace experience. In the end, it is the elders who are the best and true teachers, and the best way of learning is to sit with them for the long mornings, long afternoons, and long evenings that have been the joy of my life.

— Bev Ortiz

I would like the book to be so that people could understand it and even feel that they're doing part of it; at least, to have some part of a feeling.

— Julia F. Parker

Maggie Howard (Tabuce) peers out of an unfinished acorn granary (chuckah)
in Yosemite Valley, November 1935. Photo by Ralph Anderson, YNPRL-2044.

Acorn: Food Since The Beginning

When Julia F. Parker speaks of acorn, it is with great reverence for what the food is to her people, and for what it has been to them for centuries. Julia F. Domingues Pete Parker is Kashia Pomo from west of Santa Rosa, but she has lived most of her life in Yosemite National Park, home for generations to the Miwok/Paiute people of her husband Ralph Parker.

It is the Yosemite Miwok/Paiute acorn tradition which Julia holds so deeply in her heart, a tradition which is chronicled in the accounts of their own creation. They speak of a time when there were no people. Instead, the world was inhabited by supernatural beings, sometimes called the First People, who shared qualities of both humans and other animals.

Still remembered and revered, the First People included Coyote-man, Frog-man, Grizzly bear-woman, Lizard-man, Cougar-man and Fish-man. It is said that Coyote-man made the world.

> *When the Coyote-man had the land all finished and was ready to make the people, he went all over the land and stuck two sticks in the ground where he wished people to live and also gave the places a name. When he had all the sticks out and all the places named, he turned the sticks into men and women.*[1]

It was the First People whose acts established the ways in which the people were to live. And when they were done, their love for their creation, the people, was so great that they changed themselves into the animals of today.

1

And so they all became the animals and birds and flowers that are around us even yet.

When the people woke up and looked upon the world they found it good. They learned by watching the animals what articles were good to eat. From the grizzly bear they learned that the acorn was food. From the crane they learned to catch and eat fish. The cougar taught them that the meat of the deer, the elk, and the antelope was to be eaten. They gained wisdom from experience, by observing how the animals and birds and bugs lived. They multiplied and grew strong and built villages, even as the ants. They were happy and worshipped The Great Spirit, who had given them life, and the sun which kept them warm. And in time, out of the natural conditions surrounding them, and the accumulated wisdom of the ages, they slowly evolved a system of habits and customs, certain methods of collecting and preparing food, certain religious beliefs, and certain ideas of government.[2]

Today, sitting beneath an ancient black oak tree in Yosemite Valley, one can sense that lasting and deep-felt connection between the long ago past when the world began and the everyday present, between people and the land. It is not only there to be felt; it can be seen in the rocks and the waterfalls, which are the physical presence of the time when the world began, the time of the First People. All the great granite monoliths in the valley have meaning, have history, speak directly to those who know how to listen. For instance, some have said that the two needle-like rocks which tower to the east of Cathedral Rock are *pusi'na*, the squirrel, and *chuk'ka*, the acorn storage granary, forever reminding us of the need to store acorns where animals can't get them.[3]

It is not difficult to understand Julia's reverence for acorn if one remembers the First People and their ever-present gifts.

The Miwok/Paiute People Of Yosemite Valley

This book is about acorn, but it is also about people. To understand acorn as food, one must know something of the people who used it — who have used it for centuries — and who continue to use it today.

In 1851, the year when non-Indians first entered Yosemite Valley, the people who lived there were known as the Ahwahneechee, the people of Ahwahnee, the "valley shaped like a big mouth."[1] The Yosemite people had dual ancestry. Most appear to have been Southern Sierra Miwok-speaking people from the upper reaches of the Merced River, Mariposa Creek, and the Chowchilla and Fresno rivers; some were Mono Lake Paiute who had married into the group.[2]

Indians are known to have lived in Yosemite Valley for more than 4,000 years, and over the centuries they developed a close relationship with the land. They came to know the land's every mood intimately, and they knew the goodness that each of the seasons would reveal.

Springtime's newness meant an abundance of fresh greens to eat, both cooked and uncooked, many dried and stored for later use: the succulent stems, leaves, and flowers of miner's lettuce, the as-yet-unrolled fronds of bracken fern, the herbage of wild pea, and so many more.

Summertime brought the ripening of flower seeds, such as those of purple Clarkia, lovely farewell-to-spring, and pungent tarweed. Toward summer's end and during autumn's shortening days, blue elderberries and manzanita berries were sweetened to perfection.

In autumn there were also the "wild potatoes," like the delectable

3

bulbs of Mariposa lily, *Brodiaea*, and wild onion, all growing within the richness of Sierra soil. Fall was also time for nuts, like hazel and acorn.[3] During winter the people opened food stores and made and repaired various tools, including nets and baskets, in anticipation of the coming spring.

Throughout the year the Indians of Yosemite Valley ate the meat of deer, fish, birds such as quail and red-shafted flickers, and other animals. For hunting they used, among other things, bows and arrows, nets, decoys, blinds, traps and snares.[4]

What wasn't immediately available they got through trade. For example, the Ahwahneechee exchanged Sierran bows for Washington clamshell disk beads from the coast.[5]

And there was plenty of leisure time to enjoy the company of others. Young and old alike played games. Adults especially relished gambling games. Children's games included cat's cradle; acorn tops were among their toys.[6]

Art, creativity, and beauty were integrated into the most common of everyday things, such as baskets. While baskets were made to be used for specific and often mundane purposes, such as gathering, transporting, storing, and cooking food, they were suffused with artistic inspiration in design and construction.

The baskets also reflect the blending of the Miwok and Paiute tradition of the Ahwahneechee. While some baskets were made solely in the Southern Sierra Miwok tradition and some in the tradition of the Mono Lake Paiute, others were a skillful mixing of both, such as the acorn flour-sifting baskets made by Louisa Sam Tom, which were like the sifting baskets of the Paiute in every respect except they were rounder and flatter.[7]

It was a good life, but it wasn't idyllic. The world can be a dangerous place, and people are people. There was fear of raids by enemy groups. There were disputes to settle. These were mediated by community leaders, spiritual leaders, and the heads of family. Doctors were needed when illness struck. And, just as there were healers, there were people known as poisoners who could make people ill, even kill them, through supernatural means. For combating such illnesses, special doctors were needed.

Education was the purview of the elders and the family. Largely one-on-one, learning took place by observing, carefully listening, and eventually doing. The old-time stories, told in the wintertime, were lessons in history and social tradition; they provided a strong sense of identity and place.

Nowadays it's hard to imagine what it would be like to live so long in a small area — centuries upon centuries — with no pollution, no imminent threat to the world's survival. To do this successfully, one must have rules which affirm one's place in the world and acknowledge one's responsibility to it and each other. One such rule was to always give back for what one took. As Julia has stated, "We take from the earth. We give back to the earth. We say thank you."

The giving came through prayers, songs, good thoughts and offerings. And it came through special dance ceremonies. The dancers wore intricate featherwork and lovely shell ornaments; their dances were a visible prayer.

Another part of taking and giving is knowing how to harvest and cultivate the soil in ways that not only sustain, but increase its yield. For instance, Indians throughout California set controlled fires from time to time. These kept the ground clear of fuel that could cause a fire to spread uncontrolled. They kept the meadows free of brush and tree saplings, increased the yield of certain edible plants and fostered the growth of newly sprouted herbage so important for game animals like deer.

Plots of land were cultivated by digging for the same roots and bulbs in the same place every year or two. This loosened and aerated the soil, in turn causing the underground stems that are useful for basketry to grow straighter, the bulbs that are useful for food to become more plentiful and easier to harvest.

Some basketry plants were pruned each winter. These resprouted the following spring with vigor, yielding the long, straight shoots so essential for a strong, shapely basket. And, by the time the basket was complete, its beauty did further honor to the plant from which it came.

It was a complex relationship, that relationship with the land. California was truly a garden, nurtured and loved for generation after generation — not the wilderness many newcomers were so quick to label it.

The Mariposa Battalion

In the winter of 1851, the enduring relationship between the Yosemite Indians and the land was torn apart. In that year the first non-Indians entered Yosemite Valley with the purpose of forcing the Indians onto a reservation.

The cataclysm was forged in 1849 when a non-Indian found gold on a tributary of Agua Fria Creek, about 30 miles southeast of Yosemite. While the local Indians undoubtedly knew about the gold, they had no use for it. But its value to non-Indians caused them to flood into the Sierra foothills, quickly overrunning the area that would become Mariposa County. Conflicts developed between the Indians and the newcomers who took over the land. Some Indians made plans to reclaim their ancestral homelands from the intruders.[8]

Determined to force the Indians "on the east side of the San Joaquin and Tulare valleys, from the Tuolumne river to the Tehon [sic] Pass"[9] onto a reservation, in 1851 Governor McDougal authorized the establishment of the Mariposa Battalion, a volunteer force commanded by James D. Savage, who made a fortune by trading goods to Indians and non-Indians for gold.

The record of the Battalion's activities includes several references to acorn. At Wawona, the Battalion surprised a Southern Miwok village, and the inhabitants surrendered. While the Indians prepared to leave their village for the eventual journey to the reservation, a Battalion member decided "this a capital time to learn to eat acorn bread," which he subsequently rejected.[10]

Later, Tenieya, the headman of the Ahwahneechee, led 72 of his people to Wawona to surrender to the Battalion. Convinced there were others, Savage led the Battalion into the snow-covered valley, where they found the villages abandoned but the stores of acorn and other food full.[11]

As described by Battalion member Lafayette Bunnell in a book first published in 1880, "Their *caches* were principally of acorn, although many contained bay (California laurel), Piñon pine (Digger pine[12]), and chinquepin nuts, grass seeds, wild rye or oats (scorched), dried worms, scorched grasshoppers, and what proved to be the dried larvae of insects, which I was afterwards told were gathered from the waters of the lakes in and east of the Sierra Nevada."[13] The soldiers were certain that the people were hiding, and "It was therefore decided that the best policy was to destroy their huts and stores, with a view of starving them out, and of thus compelling them to come in and join with Tenieya and the people with him on the reservation."[14]

While the people's homes and caches were torched, Bunnell estimated the amount of stored acorn at "four to six hundred bushels."[15] By another account they reportedly "bu[rn]t over 5000 Bushels of acorns, & any quantity of old Baskets."[16] It was reported that Savage considered the sight of the charred acorns to be prettier than the valley's scenery.[17]

Soon thereafter, the Battalion left the valley, and the Ahwahneechees returned to salvage whatever burned acorns they could.[18] The following May, a Battalion detachment returned and, while searching for the people, found baskets of unshelled acorns left by the Indians on a trail near Mirror

Lake. The purported aim of this was to lead Battalion members toward a cliff from which the Indian men could hurl rocks down upon them.[19] Only one Battalion member was lured by the trap and injured, however, and in the end, the Battalion pursued the Indians to Tenaya Lake, where they surrendered and were subsequently sent to a reservation on the Fresno River.

Eventually many of the Miwok/Paiute made their way back to the valley, but the land was no longer theirs. In 1864 Yosemite Valley and the Mariposa Grove became a state preserve, the first such park. In 1890 a greatly expanded acreage became Yosemite National Park.

As tourists began to arrive in Ahwahnee in increasingly large numbers, some Miwok/Paiute found work as guides, ranch hands, and housekeepers. Some fished or gathered wild strawberries for the hotels. Much later, some became employees of the park.

This was a time of great cultural upheaval and change, as old ways blended with and gave way to new. Quilts and wool blankets replaced the old-time blankets of twisted rabbit skins. The traditional conical cedar bark house (*umucha*) began to be replaced by shake and log cabins. However, these early cabins, like the *umucha*, had a central firepit and smoke hole in the shake roof. New foods like flour and bacon, cooked in the utensils of the newcomers, largely supplanted native foods, which were still cooked in baskets.[20]

The Yosemite people now live largely as other contemporary Americans. Yet, in the whirlwind that is modern life, there are those who choose to continue the skills and traditions of their ancestors. Some still speak the language, others participate in ceremonies, and some, like Julia Parker, still make acorn.[21]

Julia with sisters and brothers, ca. 1935. Left to right: Mary Louise, Madeline, Winky, Sonny and Julia. Photographer unknown, photo courtesy of Julia F. Parker.

Julia F. Parker: The Path To Making Acorn

It requires deep commitment to practice the cultural tradition of one's ancestors, especially in a world determined to crush that tradition. Julia Parker has that commitment. She has dedicated her life to continuing the ways of both her husband's ancestors and those of her own Kashia Pomo people.

Julia expressed the force behind that commitment in 1984 when she said, "My thanks and respect are to the Miwok, Paiute, Pomo and Mono elders, Mono Lake Paiute and older people who have given me the knowledge and courage to try to carry on the true story needed in today's societies, especially for our children, grandchildren and others who are yet to be born."

Julia wants the ways of the old people to never be forgotten. It is a gift they gave her, a gift she has cherished long and dear, and such gifts must be shared. They remain to touch a place deep within the spirit of the earth and the human soul; they reveal our responsibility to the earth from which they spring so kindly. For to cook with acorn, one must create a relationship with the tree; one must understand the ground which nourishes the fruit so lovingly.

These gifts brought a sense of self and the world to Julia. The road she took to receiving them was long and tough, for she has lived in that time of great change when the old ways have been difficult to continue.

Born in the redwood hill country of Graton in Sonoma County in 1929, Julia grew up moving from tent camp to tent camp with her parents as they followed the crops, picking fruit and hops for a living.

9

Her grandmother, whom she remembers singing Indian songs and taking her out to pick clover from beneath some trees, lived with the family.

She has few recollections of these times. One vivid winter memory recalls the sound of the doorbell. When the family went to the door, they found a box of oranges left by the Salvation Army or Red Cross.

> I'll never forget that big box of oranges there sitting on that porch. And, geeee they tasted so good! Even today now I still buy boxes of oranges for my family. My grandchildren. And children.

These memories of childhood are clouded by tragedy. When Julia was only five or six, her father died. Not long after, Julia's mother, Lilly Pete, died at age 24. Lily left behind five children: Julia, the eldest; Mary Lou, a year younger; two sons, Frank and Billy; and an infant daughter, Madelaine, who was less than three months old at the time of Lilly's death.

Shortly after this, somehow or other, local social welfare authorities found the children, perhaps through their school. Separated by social welfare from their grandmother, it was unlikely the children could remain together. Children in large families usually went into different foster homes; if kept together, they ended up in orphanages.

But one of the children had tuberculosis, and a nurse was found to care for them as a foster parent. The Santa Rosa house in which this German foster mother raised them is gone now, but Julia still remembers the sleeping porch where five beds were lined up for the children. It was like sleeping out-of-doors; most of the time the porch was open, but when it was cold or rained the canvas "windows" around the porch were rolled down.

One day, Julia's foster mother loaded the children into the car and told them the first church they came to would be theirs. It turned out to be the Christian Missionary Alliance Church. Julia thought about becoming a missionary across the ocean.

The children helped earn money at odd jobs; their foster mother dropped them off at a location where a truck would pick them up and take them to work hoeing local farm fields. They also picked prunes and helped with chores at their new home, which had a family orchard, garden, and cows. In addition to milking cows, Julia cared for 50 chicks she won at the County Fair. She fed them every day, gathered their eggs, and butchered them.

Occasionally, their foster mother solicited items for the children. At

Christmas time, she introduced her "poor, little orphan Indians" at various service club parties, where they received big bagfuls of oranges, nuts, and other foods. Once, as each child came to receive a gift, a club member complained that too much was going to one family. However, their foster mother stood her ground, saying they deserved a gift and were each going to get one.

Julia feels embarrassment at how the gifts were solicited, but grateful to have received them.

> She was doing it in a good way, but then yet maybe it wasn't a good way. But I always felt what she did was good, 'cause she gave me a lot of happiness.

Despite the happiness, Julia remembers feeling isolation and shame, believing her orphan status made her different from everybody else. The feelings were magnified at the Christian Missionary Alliance Church every Mother's Day. To honor their mother, most children wore a red rose at church, but Julia was given a white rose to symbolize her mother was gone.

Julia became determined to show she was as good as anyone else. As a Campfire Girl, she worked diligently to earn awards.

> Little did I know I'd be cooking [acorn] with hot rocks, because one of the things in the Campfire Girls was to cook on a hot rock. Fry an egg on a hot rock. And I did . . . See how goofy I was.

Among Julia's responsibilities of those years was marching her siblings to school safely. In school, she admired the study habits of her Japanese-American girlfriends, and longed to speak English as well as they. However, when the children were called to give speeches about the vacations they had taken, Julia felt she didn't have anything to say. Although she knew how to raise chickens and do other farm chores, she had never been on a vacation.

Determined to get good grades like her friends, Julia decided that although she didn't have stories to tell, she could memorize and recite poems. As a result of these recitations, she achieved her goal of an "A." It was 1941, World War II had begun, and Julia was in the seventh grade.

Later that year, Julia's Japanese-American friends said goodbye and left to go to internment camps, leaving Julia with the injustice and pain of losing good friends.

I didn't have no idea about what they did to the Indian people too, see. But I felt really bad that that's not right to do that. So then I was taken out of school.

It was during the eighth grade that Julia was sent to the Bureau of Indian Affairs' Stewart Indian School in Carson City, Nevada, which she came to know as Boss Indians Around School. Her sisters and brothers were also sent.

I was just getting ready to learn the Constitution of the United States, and your rules and all that, you know. And so they took us, and when I went to the Indian school, they didn't even teach that in school. They didn't teach us our rights or anything like that . . . So it's been kind of a long struggle, when I think about what I do.

The years at Indian school assailed the pride Julia's foster mother had given her. The philosophy at Stewart was to teach students, " 'Don't be Indian. Don't sit on the ground. Don't eat acorn.' The thought is to get you away from that so you could mix in, get by in the cities, assimilate." School days here brought the pain of being called a "dirty Indian."

At Stewart, Julia went to school with about 350 Indian students from all over, between four and twenty-three years old. Perhaps the saddest part of these years was Julia's separation from her siblings. Julia, her sisters, and brothers had been together in their foster home, but now ate and lived separately. Frank and Billy lived in the small boys' dorm, Madelaine in the small girls' dorm, Mary Lou and Julia in the same big girls' dorm area, but in different buildings. As the oldest, Julia felt a responsibility to take care of the other children. She worried about the little ones especially, afraid they were sad like her and crying from loneliness, so she visited them whenever she could.

While it was an unhappy experience, the school offered a certain security, a place to stay and something to eat. There were dances, parties, and parades to organize, and Julia liked to help. In fact, by her own admission, she was "a live wire."

After meeting the school nurse and being inspired by her foster mother's occupation, Julia thought she'd like to go into nursing and wear a tidy uniform. She even spent one session of school working in the hospital, bandaging and caring for the children that came in. Since she enjoyed working with her hands and liked to help people, Julia thought of being a surgical nurse. But it was not to be.

Although Julia excelled in her classes — she met her future husband Ralph Parker in classes for "A" students they attended together — educational opportunities at the school were limited. Julia still wonders what she and other students could have become had the classes been more rigorous.

> Had we had that higher English and Math and all that we'd be doctors, lawyers. But who knows what's going to happen.
> And most of the kids that graduated from that class all managed to survive in different vocations. The girls went on to get married. Some went to nursing school and some were secretaries. And a lot of them were employed by the school itself. So then, when you went back to school, there you'd see somebody as a matron or cook. The kitchen person and all that. If I had gone back there, I probably would have been a matron.

The school was oriented toward vocational training. As one of Julia's friends put it, "You were the housecleaners of the world." And as Julia herself explained, "You were a person who was just a servant."

Students attended church regularly and received four hours a day of training in the various basics — reading, writing and arithmetic. For the boys, the other time was devoted to farming, carpentry, auto mechanics, electrical, and plumbing classes. For the girls, there was home economics, and Julia found herself in the kitchen peeling potatoes or scrubbing pots, working in the bakery, sewing, or darning socks.

The children were taught to be immaculate. Matrons oversaw their work, inspecting dresser drawers for properly folded clothes and laundry sacks to make sure clothes had been washed. Hardwood floors were scrubbed with solvent on hands and knees. A matron inspected the work, including corners, by dipping a clean, white cloth into the solvent, then rubbing it on the floor. If the cloth came out with a little dirt, the girls had to scrub the floors all over. If it came out clean, they went on to paste wax the floor by hand. This was followed by polishing with machines so big the girls could hardly keep them from getting away. In the end, the floors sparkled.

Through it all Julia maintained her independence, a strong sense of self. Girls were forbidden to play drums in the band, but Julia insisted on playing since she enjoyed the rhythms. Eventually, she was allowed to drum on the condition she be able to keep up with the boys, so she did.

Although Julia wasn't athletic, she loved sports like basketball and football and chose to become a cheerleader. Being a cheerleader was something few girls wanted to do, since they were taught in school to sit still and not to show their knees. Because of that early training about being "ladylike," to this day Julia seldom wears pants.

At the school, teasing from other children was inevitable and hard to withstand, especially when she was a new student and undergoing the unorganized, sometimes brutal initiation children will put each other through. Once, Julia was taunted with a snake. She was consumed with fright by the experience, and it took decades before her fear of snakes was replaced by respect for "those people," as she refers to snakes now.

The change came when Julia was learning to dig sedge for weaving Pomo baskets. At first, she was scared to dig because rattlesnakes sometimes lived in the sedge beds. But Julia's teacher Mabel McKay guided her hands into the sedge roots. Realizing that Mabel would put her in a safe digging area, Julia began to understand that snakes have their place in the world: "We all have our place in this society, you know. So I wasn't so afraid then."

Notwithstanding the teasing, it was fun to be together with the others. There was collective pride in the accomplishments of the school basketball team, the area's "top team." There was also a strong feeling of camaraderie. As Julia says, "We were Indian kids, you know."

Although the students were forbidden to do "Indian things," Julia was among a group of children who hid way out on campus during weekend afternoons and did "Indian things" anyway. In these small groups Julia was exposed for the first time to Paiute songs and language, as well as to traditions of other Indian people.

Unlike some of the children, Julia was poor and had no home to return to in summertime. So she stayed and worked, making what money she could, and sharing that money with her siblings. Julia also worked at various jobs throughout the school year.

She worked at the employees' club, kitchen, laundry, and office. She set tables, baked bread, cooked, sorted mail, and delivered it. She cleaned employees' houses. In the summers, she was bussed to work at farms near Reno or motels around Lake Tahoe. While working in homes, some of her shyness around strangers started to leave.

Julia bought a coat with part of her wages. Although the government issued "these old, funny coats which we'd love to have now, you know, 'cause they're all in," Julia was too proud to wear it, and went to work so she could get her own.

In 1947, the summer before her graduation, Julia came to the Yosemite home of her future husband to work in the laundry. After graduation, she returned and continued working. She sent some of the money she earned (wages were 50 to 75 cents an hour) to her siblings. She also bought them shoes and other necessities.

At Yosemite, Julia began a journey of raising a family and learning about the "old ways." At Yosemite, she had a home. Julia had been scheduled to go to a secretarial school in Oakland before moving, but her new home felt safe and secure. There were plenty of employment opportunities, and one didn't risk the chance of ending up wandering city streets. She never wanted to leave.

The years since Julia came to Yosemite have passed quickly. "I've been here 42 years," she said one day in 1990 with a laugh. "I feel like Half Dome up there! A little gray on top and a little wrinkled."

The Telles family home in Yosemite Valley, June 1941. Left to right: Helen Hogan (Coats), Beatrice Rhoan, Patricia Castro, David Telles, Helen Telles, Lucy Telles and John Telles. Photo by Ralph H. Anderson, YNPRL-2053.

The Telles Family

As part of the Parker family, Julia became like a granddaughter to Ralph's grandmother, Lucy Tom Parker Telles. Grandmother Lucy, or simply "Grandmother" as Julia came to call her, inspired in Julia a love for the old ways, especially a love for acorn. Julia's involvement with acorn is inseparable from Lucy, as Lucy's involvement was inseparable from her own past.

Lucy was the daughter of Bridgeport Tom (Mono Lake Paiute), who was born about 1850 and died in 1936, and Louisa Sam Tom (Yosemite Miwok/Paiute), who also was reportedly born before 1851.[1] Raised with strong ties to Yosemite's past, but ever a woman of the present, Lucy was a traditionalist who blended past and present with creativity.

She still made acorn the old way, with baskets, mortar, pestle, and cooking stones, but there were some changes. Cloth covered the leaching basin and metal pails replaced some of the baskets. Utilitarian baskets were made the old way, but Lucy, who was born about 1880, was among those who altered the made-for-sale basketry of her ancestors.

Among Lucy's innovations in the latter were two-color designs, "snap-in-place" lidded tops, and some completely new patterns, such as butterflies and flowers. She also made baskets of extraordinary size. One, which was three feet wide and over nineteen inches high, took four years to complete. It was exhibited at the 1939 Golden Gate International Exposition.[2]

From the 1930s until her death in 1955, Lucy demonstrated beadwork and basketry behind the Yosemite visitor center. The money she earned by selling baskets and beadwork to tourists was an essential part of the family income. As winter approached, it helped to purchase essentials, including about 100 pounds of potatoes, 100 pounds of flour, and 100 pounds of beans. Any deer the men successfully hunted were made into jerky.

Mrs. Telles was the leader of a large, extended family, and a hard worker for whom the needs of others were always uppermost. Julia remembers her with great love and admiration:

> *To me she was a very caring person. She always thought about the grandchildren. She'd go downtown and bring back something to eat. Food or something. Bananas or oranges or stuff like that. She raised I don't know how many grandsons. She only had one granddaughter. And she was always cooking, and washing, and cleaning for those boys . . . And then when I came along, I stepped in and helped with the fellows' cooking.*
>
> *I'll never forget her. We used to iron galvanized tubfuls of shirts by hand. She was a working woman.*

Lucy's voice was quiet, never demanding, "but you just listened," Julia recalls. She was someone you could count on. There were times when Julia and her young children lived alone because her husband was working for the Park Service out of the area. With her husband gone, Julia turned to Lucy for companionship.

> *She was always the one you could go and sit with and be with. And she'd protect you, too.*

Lucy Tom Parker Telles was married twice. Her first marriage was to Jack Parker (Paiute), with whom she had two sons, David and Lloyd, who was the father of Julia's husband, Ralph. Tragically, Jack died when Lloyd was only four years old. Twelve years later Lucy married John Telles (Mexican-American from Texas), with whom she had another son, Johnny, Jr., in 1922. She also had a daughter, Hazel.

John Telles worked for Curry Company, the park concessionaire at that time, as a houseman and janitor. Because of his work, John brought home cast-off clothing and linens, from which Lucy sewed quilts and coats. Sometimes he brought acorns home.

At various times, Lucy and John shared their home with their children and grandchildren. Family members also lived in other nearby homes. The houses were in a circular cluster of thirteen three-room cabins built by the Park Service and known as the "Indian Village." The upper exterior of each house was shingle-sided, the lower vertical board and batten. The roofs were double-pitched.

Previously, the Yosemite Miwok/Paiute lived at an old village site near the present-day hospital. The housing there consisted of canvas-covered framework. The Park Service denied requests to make improvements to these houses and instead moved the people to the Indian Village. Here, Lucy chose a house above the floodplain.

A desire to segregate seems to have governed the location of the Indian Village, driven by the same prejudice that caused Indians to be buried in a separate area of Yosemite Valley's "pioneer graveyard," away from non-Indians. Built in the mid '30s and destroyed in the late '60s (one house moved to the park corporation yard still stands), the Village kept Yosemite's native people away from other residents and most tourists. Sometimes tour bus guides would point out the Indian children and announce that they might "do a little dance." After the children made the mock dance that was expected of them, the tourists would throw them money.

The new houses had two nine by twelve-foot bedrooms and a nine by sixteen-foot dining/kitchen area with cold running water. Water was heated by woodstove. A central restroom/shower facility was shared by everyone.

When Julia first came to work in Yosemite in 1947, she lived in one of these houses with her future father-in-law, Lloyd Parker, and his niece. Ralph's mother had died when he was four, so Lucy had raised him. Traditional rules dictated that a wife did not speak to her father-in-law for a while after marrying, so the newlyweds moved into John and Lucy's home for about a year.

Shortly after the birth of their first child in 1949, Julia and Ralph moved into their own Indian Village home. Every two weeks $12, a sizeable portion of their income, was taken out of Ralph's paycheck for rent, but it was manageable since there was no electricity or telephone bill, and they didn't have a car. By 1963, they would have a new, larger home made by putting two Village cabins together.

Julia never left Yosemite during her first few years in the Valley, not even to shop. She was concerned about the children, and necessities could be bought through the Montgomery Ward catalogue. Members of the Tabucco family, who had a grocery store in Mariposa, would periodically come to sell appliances. The Watkins man came with spices to sell the women for their cakes and cookies, and Lifesavers candies to give to the children.

The Kirby man even came to sell vacuums. Although there were no rugs to vacuum, Julia remembers that if one person bought a vacuum, everyone did, and these were on sale for $75. So they opened up a charge account and paid off their bill at $5 a month.

When her husband was away working, Julia would pack some sandwiches and take the children to a beach on the Merced River to practice diving off a rock and swimming. As the newest member of the Telles' extended family, she also spent much of her time helping Lucy and her granddaughter Helen with family chores. There was always a lot of work to be done providing for everyone's needs. Many a time four and five long lines of drying, laundered shirts stretched between the pine trees.

Initially, Lucy did all the laundry using a washboard propped inside a galvanized tub. Later, the boys purchased a wringer machine. Still later, a machine complete with spinner was purchased, but Lucy never liked it. Because there were so many shirts to wash, it wouldn't work half the time.

Julia and Helen helped with the ironing and, while working in the park laundry, they brought the family wash with them to clean and iron on their lunch hour, insuring that the men of the house had spic, span, and starched shirts to wear.

With so many people to feed, stew was a mainstay of everyone's diet. Once the boys encouraged Julia to ask Lucy to buy steak for them. Lucy agreed, but being a thrifty and fair-minded woman, she cut the steak into chunks to make a stew for everyone. The boys were disappointed.

There was always a pot of good, rich coffee brewing on the Telles stove in anticipation of company. From her home across the way, Julia could see company arrive. Immediately, she headed over to help, for no matter what time of day company came, Lucy would prepare a meal to feed her guests before the visiting commenced.

Except in poor weather, Lucy spent most of her time out-of-doors next to her house, by the family firepit where she heated the stones needed to cook her acorn. Next to this rock-ringed campfire circle was a grill made by mounting a flat cast-iron slab on rocks, close to the ground. Here Lucy could be found almost every day by eight in the morning, having her coffee, weaving a basket, or making stew, yeast bread, tortillas, and other food.

A community feeling permeated the Indian Village. On weekends people gathered to share big potluck meals. They sat around a bonfire and sang "49er songs" backed by guitar, banjos, and violins. On birthdays, or if there was a death, people came from all over.

When someone passed on, people were invited to a "cry." Everyone congregated at the home of a relative of the deceased to show respect. Five men stood and sang traditional songs thoughout the night. Men and women danced to the *a cappella* singing while holding dresses, shoes, and other articles that belonged to the deceased. Their feet made a step and slide motion as they danced in a circle around a bonfire, breaking every so often to rest and eat before proceeding anew.

Everyone participated. Although Julia wasn't sure what to expect at her first cry, she found out she didn't need to be taught what to do. "You just participate," she said. When the sun came up, the person's clothes and other personal belongings were thrown into the fire and burned.

The mourning songs brought Julia's mind back many years. She saw her grandmother sitting near a fire burning clothes and realized the songs she recalled her grandmother singing were songs of mourning for Julia's father.

Despite the cries, Julia's memories of the Indian Village are good. They include the sight and smell of huge sheetcakes, oatmeal cookies, and raisin cookies Lucy baked to perfection. And she remembers Lucy making acorn. Acorn was not an everyday food for Lucy, but something she made for special occasions; everyone in the community was invited to share in its goodness.

Clear memories remain of Lucy as a woman in her 70s, climbing to the top of a rock nearly 17 feet high to pound acorn — a rock from which Lucy could see everything that was going on, but not be seen herself. Today, walking past that rock brings tearful memories to Julia. Lucy died in 1955, but Julia can still recall the sound made by the rock as Lucy pounded. Every rock makes a distinctive sound, and this one resonates through Julia's mind.

Memories come flooding in at unexpected times. Helping to roll dough to make frybread for a community gathering once sparked the memory of a lesson that nothing should be wasted. The lesson came when Julia was making yeast bread:

> *Lucy would never allow me to leave any flour in the pan. Once, I was rolling it and said I'm through. And she said, "No you're*

*not. Look at all that flour. You're wasting it." So she showed me
how to get all that flour off of that pot . . . You don't waste
anything.*

Lucy Telles was compassionate and devoted. She reminded Julia of
her mother and served as inspiration for Julia in raising her own family
and carrying on with acorn making.

*She was a busy lady, and I guess you might say I used her as a
role model. That woman was up at the crack of dawn cooking,
washing, and making her own [yeast] bread.*

Now Julia works in the Yosemite Indian Museum surrounded by these
memories. Photographs of Lucy and other elders who have influenced
Julia are mounted on the museum wall. Glass cases contain baskets made
by Lucy and the women who came to visit at Lucy's house all those
years ago. Behind the museum, in the same area where Lucy once demonstrated basketry and beadwork, Julia is among those who have been hired
by the Park Service to make acorn for park visitors to taste.

In the museum, Julia sits on a low platform, talking to visitors while
using some traditional skill or another: making a basket, a netted bag of
natural fiber, a miniature doll, all following Indian tradition and the
dictates of Julia's own creativity. There is an endless stream of people
through the museum, but Julia is unflappable.

Today Julia's words flow easily, without self-consciousness, as she explains Yosemite Miwok/Paiute culture to museum visitors, but this was
not always so. There was a time when she felt intimidated by lack of
education. Now, years later, she patiently answers every question, no
matter how out of context, with grace and humor.

She is gratified by people's acceptance and willingness to learn. She is
heartened by the opportunity to share a little of what she knows.

In an attempt to touch the hearts of the visitors with her culture, Julia
tells stories. On one particular day, she recalled a deer-hunting trip with
her husband. Her voice was quiet but animated; her hands delicately,
painstakingly fashioning a basket all the while.

Changes in the story's action and emphasis were expressed with only
the slightest difference in pitch. The listeners were drawn in by the
momentum of the passion in Julia's voice, losing themselves in the magic
of the words.

Through the words, we were carried through the silent, patient task of tracking a deer, crawling on hands and knees over rocks and through the thick chaparral.

> *And usually women don't go. They stay away. In today's world we don't want him to get lost, although he would never get lost. But he said he wanted me to drive for him. . . .*
>
> *And then I was supposed to meet him. And he gave me all these signs. What to do. How I should wait for him and look for him. So in the meantime when I was out waiting for him I was out scouting the plants . . . when I came across what I call that chaparral. It was in the fall time. I said, "I wonder if that is good for baskets?" So I picked some up and started splitting it. Here it was just strong stuff. It was just good. So that's how I found out about the chaparral.*
>
> *So then he was — when I walked with him, he was so quiet. And I go "blahblahblahblahblah." My whole voice was going. And he said, "Shhhhhh." He says, 'The deer will hear you.' I said, "Ohhh-kay." So then I'd go along, and I'd crunch along in the brush. And he'd say, "Shhhhhh." . . . The next day he said, "You know, Julia. That was the best time I ever had with you. You never talked."*

Julia laughed heartily at the remembrance, then continued with her story.

> *'Cause I was just busy watching him. And it felt like he was in the old days. I could just see him with his bow. 'Cause he likes to bow hunt too. But he can't do bow and rifle. So he chose rifle . . .*
>
> *And so anyway he spotted those tracks. And he said, "That deer followed us Julia." He said, "They're really smart." He was following us.*
>
> *And one time my husband took my older son out, and they went hunting. And he stood on top of a ridge. It was really neat. He'd find a high rock. And he would stand there on that rock, and he looked all around him. It was beautiful to see the way his actions, and the way he carried himself. Respectful and wanting to get his game, and not getting frustrated if he didn't get it.*
>
> *And then he lucked out. He found one that was in the chaparral.*

In the end, Ralph's patience was rewarded with success. And we, the listeners, were rewarded for our patience in turn as we were trusted with a tender revelation:

> *And [Ralph] says, "I want to show you something." So then I said, "What do you want to show me?" And he says, "Come here." So the path went down in this canyon like. And then there was a spring in there. And I said, "Oh, gee. Water and all. A spring." "And up on top," he said, "the deer comes there to drink." He knew that because there's a lot of tracks. So right above that spring there was this beautiful pounding rock. . . .*
>
> *And it was a beautiful flat rock and the pestle was still sitting in it! And I had gone by it. And he had gone by it. And he found it. He knew I liked to see things like that. And so we looked at it. And it was just like that person who was in there pounding acorn had heard us coming and just disappeared into the bushes. We just left it in there.*
>
> *It was the most prettiest sight to see that. I said a little prayer, and I just left it there. I didn't touch it. Because that wasn't mine. Because when women pound their acorn they each have their own rock. They have to find their own rock.*

Julia has raised four children and has assisted with the education and upbringing of two granddaughters and seven grandsons. Ever since her children were small, she has also educated thousands of strangers in the ways of the Yosemite Miwok/Paiute.

She has done all this with boundless enthusiasm and unwavering energy tempered by measured calmness. For despite family and community responsibilities, working at the museum, and quiet, one o'clock-in-the-morning hours spent making baskets, traditional dolls, soaproot brushes, string, ornaments, or game pieces, Julia follows the elders' teachings that the old ways, as with life itself, must not be rushed.

It's hard to fathom such a busy life, but then one remembers Julia's mentor, Lucy Tom Parker Telles: the woman who did what needed to be done, who was always there when you needed her. And one can't help but think that Grandmother is looking with approval at Julia from her photograph on the wall at the Indian Museum.

Julia F. Parker: Continuing The Path

In Yosemite Julia always worked. For several years, she worked cleaning people's homes, bringing along the children who weren't yet in school. Julia still remembers the time she thought a home she'd cleaned was spotless, but it was pointed out she hadn't dusted the books in their case. Another time, she was asked to help the same woman, who had a patio and outdoor barbeque, to scrub and wax the granite rocks nearby. Julia later decided the rocks around her own fireplace could use such a waxing.

The path that led Julia to her work demonstrating acorn making was a long one. An unexpected impetus came when Grandmother Lucy died and the National Park Service asked Julia to carry on the demonstrations behind the Visitor Center. Julia felt it was not her place to do this. She was not born in the area. She didn't yet know how to make a basket.

When Julia had watched Grandmother Lucy weave in those early years, she never imagined herself making baskets. Raising children is fully involving, and Grandmother had told her this was not the time to learn basketry.

Instead, Lucy taught her beadwork, and Julia supplemented her income by making tiny pins with beaded leather shoes for Lucy and neighbor Chris Brown to sell to park visitors. Chris, who demonstrated traditional dance, circulated among visitors with the shoes pinned to a black, felt cowboy hat.

Julia decided to accept the half-time work as cultural demonstrator when nobody else was available to take the job, and she received assurance that she would be able to have her children with her. First, however, she set out to finally learn basketry.

To understand early-day methods of making acorn, one must in turn understand the baskets. While few people cook acorn with baskets today — it simply isn't practical — baskets were essential tools in earlier days, and they were an integral part of the people's daily life.

An average old-time Central California Indian household had some 20 different types of baskets which served a variety of utilitarian functions, including food gathering, storage, processing, cooking, and serving; cradling babies; general storage; animal trapping; and carrying wood and other items. They were also given as gifts.

To learn basketry, Julia first consulted library books, but they weren't of any help, so she turned to the well-known basket makers in the area. She learned in the traditional way, by quietly watching and listening to them. Just as the old ways take time and patience, so does the learning, which occurs a little at a time. The teachers know how serious their student is by how well she perseveres through the tests of learning.

Julia's path took her to Mono Lake Paiute weaver Minnie Mike, her sister Carrie Bethel, their half sister Sadie McGowan, and Lula Hess. It took her to Tina Charlie (Mono Lake Paiute), a woman in her 80s who spoke no English, so Julia's Miwok- and Paiute-speaking father-in-law acted as an interpreter. She also went to Nellie Charlie, Tina's sister, and Ida Bishop (Northfork Mono).

The "ladies" taught Julia how to know when the willow used in the baskets was right for gathering. They showed her how to split it into sewing strands for Paiute-style baskets. The willow was difficult to work with but, as Julia learned, "If you can master willow, you can master anything."

Carrie Bethel showed Julia how to start a basket and how to put it together. Later, Julia learned that there are many kinds of starts, and that it is possible to tell where a basket comes from by how it is started. She noticed that Carrie used a sewing strand that looked different from the willow she knew. It turned out to be split and trimmed sedge rhizome.

Julia took many trips to visit the ladies, and she found out about redbud. She began buying coils of redbud and learning how to use it. At first it kept cracking and breaking, but she continued on.

Next she learned about bracken fern root and how to gather it when the leaves turn yellow. She learned that the plant talks to you, telling you when it's ready. She would wander up a river trying to find the fern, pulling up various plants, looking for the one with black colored roots. Later, she learned that the sewing strands aren't naturally black, you have to dye them. Rusty tin cups, rusty nails, and acorn are among the items Julia places in a water-filled rusty bucket or cast iron skillet with the basketry plants she wishes to dye.

She also learned about deer grass (*Muhlenbergia*), used by the Western Mono for the foundation in coiled baskets. And the learning never stopped.

She learned to make each willow warp the same size by sliding a loop of knotted string along it, scraping it with a knife to a smooth, rounded size that would fit through the loop. Decades later, from Pomo weaver Mabel McKay, Julia learned about taboos which dictate that a woman must never weave during her menstrual period, and must not weave when she is unhappy. Each weaver had rules to follow which came from her own cultural heritage.

Now, Julia can look at a rod of the right kind of willow and see baskets in it. Small willow rods become little acorn mush boilers in her mind. Big willow rods become big mush boilers. And when she looks at someone else's basket, she has respect for the hands that worked on it, a knowledge that has come from quietly listening, watching, and learning to shape her own baskets out of the basket plants.

Julia works patiently, gathering each plant in the proper season, often from the traditional places revealed to her by Lucy Telles. In the fall she travels to Mono Lake for willow shoots. She trades for sedge from the Northfork Mono. She cuts her redbud in the winter on the lower Merced River, and she finds bracken fern rhizomes in the late summer. Then she takes the plants, cleans and stores them for at least six months, resoaks and reworks them to the proper size, and begins to weave.

And always, she works with gratitude for the elders. As Julia has stated, "I owe my skill and knowledge given to me by my basket maker friends; the working, and making friends with the willow, sedge, grasses, and redbud." Her goal is to give back to the people what the grandmothers gave to her.

The lessons taught by the elders remain firm in Julia's mind: "Gather willow when the leaves turn yellow." "Scrape the willow till it sings to you." "Borrow, don't steal, the way of fellow basket maker friends." "Don't forget old way, Julia." "Take from the earth and say please." "Give back to the earth and say thank you." "Listen to the basket makers who have gone before you."

Julia's baskets have travelled to such distant places as the Smithsonian Institution in Washington, D.C., and Oslo, Norway. And on March 6, 1983, Julia had the honor of presenting England's Queen Elizabeth II with a basket which represented untold hours of her dedicated labor. The basket is now displayed in the queen's museum.

Julia made her presentation to the queen in the grand style of an ambassador, dressed in the ceremonial finery worn by Yosemite people for generations — a pale blue, late 1800s-style dress hand-stitched by Julia, a belt decorated with abalone pendants, clamshell disk bead and trade bead necklaces, and a headband with abalone pendants. At her side, she had granddaughter Tisina, age six.

This moment was a long time coming. When Julia first started working as a demonstrator in 1960, a ranger introduced her to the public.

> And he'd always say, "Well Julia is out there in the back . . .
> She'll answer your questions, if you ask." People would come
> out there. And I wouldn't say too much. And then they'd ask
> me something. Then I'd have to talk, because it was part of my
> job. So the last time he came, I said to him, "Remember when I
> used to hide behind my basket?" And he laughed.

Initially, the job as demonstrator was two hours in the morning and two in the afternoon, so Julia also worked at the Ahwahnee Hotel gift shop.

> I was the first Native American girl to work in the Ahwahnee — of
> any color to work in the Ahwahnee. We had to be dressed up in
> suits and everything, you know. So at one time I was well suited . . .
> But anyway, you stand up there, and she [the supervisor]
> didn't want me to work behind the counter. And so she'd put
> me in the corner where all the Indian things were. So I just had
> to stand there . . . like the wooden Indian; just stand there and
> answer questions about baskets, and things, and all that.

One day, when an employee was absent, Julia was finally trained at the register. Because she knew the product, sales were good, and Yosemite Park and Curry Company management decided to open an Indian store, the Pohono shop, with an inventory that was half composed of park mementos. Julia agreed to manage it on the condition that her staff would be Indian.

In making this request, Julia was remembering a conversation with a young woman who was among those bussed from Sherman Institute

Indian School to work in Yosemite Valley. Although qualified to do computer and secretarial work, the woman could only get work as a maid. Julia recalls telling her, "I think that they think that all you girls are just housecleaners." Now Julia could do something about it. Julia taught herself to balance the day's receipts and order inventory by studying previous ledger books. The young women needed no training in selling and keeping the shop clean. In fact, Julia learned a lot by listening to each one talk about the products of her own cultural area.

Despite the good work everyone did, Julia still could not get full-time employment at the shop, so when she was offered a full-time, summer seasonal position as a demonstrator, she took it.

> *And I said, "Okay. I would rather do this over here." So I didn't work for Curry anymore. See it was — what you had in those days, you had to say, "I want to do it" or, you know, they molded you. You're a housecleaner. And there's nothing wrong with that. And if I retire, I mean that's what I'll do. I'll go clean and wash dishes or something, because I love to make things clean and neat.*

Looking back on her years of becoming a demonstrator and learning basketry, Julia muses that perhaps it was her own roots she was seeking in the willows. She always loved to work with her hands, whether sewing, cooking, or cleaning. Through the baskets and her work as a cultural demonstrator, she was not only using her hands, but she was coming home to her own Indian heritage.

Julia Parker, 1949, with her daughter Virginia Parker in a cradleboard woven by Lucy Telles. Photo by Ralph Parker, courtesy of Julia F. Parker.

Learning To Make Acorn

Julia saw acorn being prepared for the first time in Yosemite in 1949. It's now unclear whether it was Lucy or her sister Alice that was leaching the flour, but Julia vividly remembers what she thought.

> . . . I saw the sand bed laid out. And she had all the flour in there, and I stood and I said, "What's that?" I think I told them, "What's that?" And then they said, "Well, don't you know? That's acorn." See, so I just shut up then. Because I didn't know about it, so I had better be quiet. Rather than say, "Where do you get the acorn? What do you do with that? How and all this?" I just kept quiet. And then after a while [I learned].

Acorns were especially plentiful in Yosemite that year. Autumn found Julia joining Grandmother Lucy, who had a car, on gathering expeditions. They picked acorns off the ground and put them into baskets, then transferred them into gunnysacks for the trip home.

Joining the two women was Julia's firstborn, Virginia, comfortably wrapped in a cradleboard basket Lucy wove. Grandmother showed Julia how to lean the basketed baby against a tree, from where the baby could watch them gather. As Julia fondly recalls, "When I think about it now it felt like old-time ways that I was doing. Here we are, out gathering acorn, with the baby in the basket content, sleeping, playing, looking at the leaves, and all that."

When Julia thinks of Lucy now, she remembers the sound of acorn being pounded. Lucy wouldn't announce her task; she would just sit

Julia climbing atop the nearly 17-foot rock where she and Lucy Telles used to pound acorn.

quietly and start working. From her home early in the morning, Julia would awaken to the steady rhythm of rock against acorn flour, then get ready to join Lucy.

Eventually, Julia stopped waiting for the sound of pounding. She knew where Grandmother would be, so she just got ready and went. As she recalls, "I was kind of a curious person. I guess I had to be curious, to go over there and want to learn, to watch what she was doing. I never missed a thing."

Julia's learning took place in the same manner as that of countless generations before her: one on one, they watched the process until they

Julia spent a special morning atop the same rock recently. In preparation for winnowing acorn, she's splitting a groove in shelled nuts with an obsidian flake (the old way). The baskets and looped stirrer were all made by Lucy Telles.

were old enough to try. They didn't question the methods, knowing that the ladies knew the best way to make acorn, and knowing it had been passed down through generations of grandmothers. "If you sit and listen to them, you learn it," says Julia, who is saddened that this way of learning seems to have all but disappeared.

Grandmother had three rocks where she pounded. When she was by herself early in the morning, she pounded on a special, low-to-the-ground rock. It was the sound of this rock that reverberated through Julia's mind as she slept in her own home.

When she and Grandmother wanted to pound without interruption, they climbed atop a rock nearly 17 feet high with four or five mortar holes. Eventually, other young women got interested and began to help with the pounding on a third bedrock mortar, close to the ground and with many holes.

As the ladies worked they shared talk, teasing, and laughter amidst the rhythmic thud of stone pestles against acorn. Sometimes seven or eight women worked on the same rock, usually three.

At times, cries of "Rock!" permeated the scene. This was a spirited reminder to any woman who inadvertently allowed the cushion of acorn between mortar and pestle to grow too small that it was time to add more acorn. Otherwise, the pestle might strike directly against the mortar, causing stone grit to enter the food.

Their work began around eight o'clock in the morning and continued until two or three o'clock in the afternoon. Time passed quickly and pleasantly, interrupted only by lunch, which was often brought to the work site by a grandchild or another woman.

Huge quantities of acorn were necessary to feed the Indian community at special events and, as a family leader, Grandmother was the supplier. It took two days to make enough. The first day was absorbed in pounding and sifting. As the women pounded, Lucy checked to see if the acorn was ready to sift.

Although Julia was interested in sifting, this was a specialty. It was Lucy's job. Sifting was the most difficult part, and Lucy wanted to make sure none of the food was wasted. She wanted to make sure they learned the right way, the special way.

As Julia explained, "I think she was being very, very conservative and didn't want us to shake the flour all around. 'Cause you know when you're learning how it flipflops all over."

The next day was devoted to leaching in the morning, and cooking in the afternoon. At each step — gathering, pounding, sifting, winnowing, and cooking — the women used baskets which Lucy had made. They also used Grandmother's looped stirrers, which were specially made for pulling the cooking rocks out of the acorn.

Lucy always cooked large amounts of acorn. She used about 6 pounds of leached acorn flour to make acorn mush in a basket she wove which stood 13 inches high, 16 inches across at its base, and 19 inches across on top. The mush was transferred by bowlfuls into a galvanized tub filled three-quarters full of cold water, where it congealed into acorn biscuits. Lucy also used about 4 pounds of leached acorn flour to make soup in the same basket. Julia notes that it was an "eight-rock basket;" eight heated stones were necessary to cook its contents, which filled 9 inches of its height, to proper consistency.

In August of 1990 Kathleen Smith (Bodega Miwok/Dry Creek Pomo) and I journeyed with Julia to the site of the Indian Village to see the rocks where Julia and Lucy once pounded, and the homesites where the Parker and Telles families once lived. The area was shaded by the branches of yellow pines, black oaks, canyon live oaks, incense cedar trees, and an occasional Douglas fir, some new, others there with Julia 20 years earlier. Lucy had gathered acorns from several of the nearby black oaks, including a large oak in what was once her yard. The ground was covered with leaves, which cushioned our steps and crunched as we walked.

Signs of previous habitation seemed few, but at every turn Julia found something: non-native myrtle still growing where it had been planted in gardens with once-tended lawns, the depression of the roadbed, bed springs, a car axle, the fire hydrant that once stood in the middle of the cluster of houses, Lucy's homesite, and, of course, numerous bedrock mortars.

We located the small, somewhat portable mortar over two feet across where Lucy started her pounding. It stood a few steps from her home; from here, she could watch the house while she worked.

The rock was brought from elsewhere by Lucy's father, Bridgeport Tom. Heavy as it is, Julia speculated he might have used horses to pull it in. Once, she considered moving the stone to her present Yosemite Valley home, but concluded, "No. It's her rock. It belongs there."

Its mortar hole was shallow, with a depression so imperceptible that it would be unrecognizable as a pounding rock to most. Lucy didn't need to pound in a deep hole; in fact, it appears she objected to the deeper ones.

Julia supposes Lucy preferred shallow mortars because they were the same as those she'd seen her elders use. Such mortars work well with the stout, river rounded rock pestles the ladies used. Deeper holes require the lean, elongated pestles used in other areas and, in Julia's experience, cause the oily black oak acorns to become packed together in the bottom of the mortar during pounding.

After Lucy had pounded some acorn at her rock, she'd invite other women to go to a bigger bedrock, 10 by 12 feet across and low to the ground. The rock was close to a home, yet secluded. As with all the mortars in the area, its holes had been there long before the Indian Village was established.

Julia now carefully cleared off an accumulation of leaves, looking for the tiny indentation where she once pounded, laughed, and enjoyed the company of the ladies. She had chosen her depression thoughtfully, based upon the shallow size that Lucy used.

One by one, we cleared the organic debris away to reveal several holes, all spaced on the flat bedrock so that several women could pound there at once. Some were extraordinarily deep compared to those Julia used, so I asked her about them. Although uncertain of their purpose, she speculated they might have been for pounding medicinal herbs.

Before leaving, we placed pine needles and oak leaves atop the holes. "When we left, we always covered them up," Julia said, thinking back. This protected the holes until it was time to clean and use them again.

Eventually, we came to the huge bedrock boulder, jutting nearly 17 feet above the ground surface, where Lucy would pound if she had help. Secluded and shaded, with an exquisite, expansive view, this rock offered privacy, a place to work without interruption. From the top one could look out over the entire village and beyond while watching the children play below.

Often, Julia and Lucy pounded atop this rock together. They pushed and dragged about 25 pounds (two small sackfuls) of acorn to the top in preparation for their work.

We struggled to the top of the rock, with its nearly vertical walls, to find the mortars where Julia and Lucy once worked. To help us reach the top, Julia picked up some small boulders and placed them atop a ledge on the back side of the rock. Stepping onto first the ledge, then the boulders, and finally finding small foot- and handholds on its upper heights, Kathleen was able to make the top, afterward extending a hand to us.

It was hard to imagine how lithe and energetic Grandmother must have been to make her way to the top while in her 70s, albeit with help. But the feeling of exhilaration at our success and the beauty of the view were amply rewarding.

"I've had 30 years to think about it. Watch it. Sitting by myself at a pounding rock. This is the best time to make acorn."

— Julia F. Parker

Strict Attention To Detail

Watching Julia prepare acorn, one appreciates her precise and careful methods. The process is laden with subtleties. It requires strict attention to detail. As Julia notes about the elders she observed, "The ladies, when they did their acorn, they were very, very particular." It is this "particularness," this keen attention to detail and the proper way of doing things, that guides Julia's acorn making from beginning to end.

The elders taught that there were rules which must be followed. Wishing for acorns was bad. You never looked at the nuts in the trees lest they be scared away, and a poor acorn harvest result. Instead, you waited for them to fall. Then they must be gathered with the utmost respect, or there would be no acorn in future years.

Sometimes, as Julia looks out the window of her second floor office, she inadvertently spots an acorn in a tree. Quickly she glances away, thinking, "Oh! It saw me. I didn't see it!" Other times Ralph mentions to her that it looks like it's going to be a good year for acorns. Thinking of the ladies' rules she tells him, "I'm not going to look for them in the trees!"

In 1942 "Junior Park Naturalist" C.C. Presnall described an acorn festival he witnessed on Sunday, October 4, 1931. It was reportedly the first such gathering in Yosemite in nine years.[1] About 50 Indians attended the festival, which began on October 1. On that night and the two following, the acorn dance was held.

Most participants abstained from food for the duration of the event, which was hosted to give thanks and dedicate the year's new acorn

37

harvest before any was eaten. On the third day, ten specially chosen women pounded the acorn into flour using mortar and pestle. Then they leached away its tannic acid in four large sand basins. The following morning the acorn was cooked with heated stones. Children tasted the cooked acorn that adhered to the stones when they were removed from the cooking basket. Nearby, men prepared steaks over a campfire.

Then, a final dance was announced from the ceremonial house. Kneeling around the fire, the participants sang a special song accompanied by split stick clappers and cocoon rattles, after which head dancer Chris Brown gave an oration, inviting the spirits of their ancestors to come and eat. He threw meal into the air for this purpose.

The dancing, an elegant, rhythmic, visible prayer, continued inside, after which the dancers were led out of the ceremonial house and around the fire where the cooking stones had been heated. Everyone who planned to eat the acorn was invited to join this dance, which culminated with an elder woman offering acorn four times around the fire, to be carried in the four directions to the spirits.

More dancing followed:

> These dances were chiefly expressions of thanks for the abundant acorn crop, and petitions for an equally large crop next year. There was a fire dance for the fire that heated the cooking stones; a stone dance for the stones that cooked the meal; and a basket dance for the baskets in which it was cooked. Then there were dances to the "First People," who made the world, and especially to "Coyote-Man," one of the most important of the "First People."

Respect is integral to the old ways. According to Julia, "We in Yosemite have a feeling about our acorn. When the acorn does come, there's dances and songs. We take from the earth, we give back to the earth, and we say thank you." By the time Julia lived at the Indian Village, the kind of dances Presnall described were no longer being held, but acorn was still prayed for, as Julia continues to pray for it today.

For Julia and the other Indians at the village, the very act of appreciating acorn and using it was an act of respect, of giving back. They prayed when they gathered, prepared, and shared the food. A handful of cooked acorn was offered to the fire in a prayerful way, usually by the woman in charge of its making. Sometimes it was thrown into the fire in the four directions. Then the people ate.

Julia also has a special way to approach a mortar that has stood unused in which she would like to pound:

> *I find myself saying a little prayer. You know, "May I use it? I know you want me to use it." That's what I do; that's how I approach it. And I don't think that that person is gone. It's there and it needs to be used.*

Acorn and California Indians

There is no such thing as "California Indian acorn making." First, not all California Indian groups used acorn, and among those groups who did, the quantities, species, and processing methods varied.

Not only do the details of preparation vary from group to group, they sometimes vary among families, and even from person to person. The closer we look the more we can appreciate the artistry and skill with which people have adapted the techniques to meet the needs of place.

Julia's techniques are specific to the Yosemite Miwok/Paiute. Here the versatile black oak acorn is preferred for its availability, taste, color, flavor, storage capability, and thickening properties. By percent, black oak (*Quercus kelloggii*) acorns contain 31.4% water, 3.44% protein, 13.55% fats, 8.60% fiber, and 41.81% carbohydrate, making them an exceedingly nutritious food.

Sixteen species of oaks are found in California. The deciduous black oak is especially abundant. It is found within about 18% of the state, from about 200 to 8,000 feet in elevation. Black oaks grow in the mountains and hills of northern California, the Coast Ranges as far south as San Diego, and throughout the Sierra Nevada foothills.

Black oak acorns take two years to fully develop and, in good years, each tree can produce between 200 and 300 pounds. Along with tanbark oak (*Lithocarpus densiflora*), which bears acorns but is not considered a true oak by present-day botanists, black oak acorns have always been the most preferred by California Indians.[2]

Maggie Howard returning from gathering acorns in Yosemite Valley, 1930.
Photo by Bert Harwell, YNPRL-1963.

Gathering

When the leaves turn yellow, Grandmother Lucy taught, it's acorn gathering time. Acorns fall from the trees twice each season. The first fall consists of unhealthy, worm- and insect-infested acorns, and it is left alone.

Winds bring the others down later, in late September or early October depending on the weather. These good, healthy acorns are heavier than the others, a quality that is felt for as they are gathered off the ground. Each acorn is also inspected by sight and felt for any bumps or holes. The flawed acorns are left on the ground to return to the earth or be eaten by squirrels and birds.

Depending on the weather, some years are better for acorn than others; a plentiful harvest only occurs every four or five years, but individual trees can vary.

As Julia has observed, the number of deer seen in Yosemite Valley in autumn is an indication of how good a given year's harvest will be. More deer come into the valley when acorn isn't plentiful at the higher elevations. During such years, Julia finds herself picking acorns off the ground with deer close by.

In off years, when there wasn't enough acorn, Lucy used to purchase it already pounded from Ida Bishop. Even in such years, however, it was still important to go out and gather at least one basketful of acorns. As Julia explains, "The elders told me when it comes get out and pick and gather, even if it's one basketful, so the acorn spirit will know you're happy for the acorn, and next year the acorn will come."

41

Care is taken to gather only healthy acorns.

Julia never talks of "collecting" acorn or other natural material. Instead, she makes a thoughtful distinction between collecting and gathering. "Indians gather," she states with conviction. "Most non-Indians collect."

The distinction lies in intent: gathering implies respectfully taking only what you need and respectfully giving back for what you take. To Julia, collecting implies a more wanton, thoughtless hoarding, with no attention paid to the method used or quantity taken.

It is only by gathering responsibly that one guarantees the future harvest. And the best and most responsible gathering techniques are those learned from others; Julia's techniques have changed because of her teachers.

> *I used to gather the great big acorns, you know, just like the biggest orange or biggest apple. And one of the ladies says, "You know that it will take longer to dry, Julia. Go for the littler ones." So then I started picking up those littler ones. And they dry faster.*

Each woman had a special acorn tree handed down through generations. Paiute elder Maggie Howard (Tabuce) had just such a tree, a tree which would usually produce lots of nuts. Tabuce's tree is actually a cluster of three trees which stand adjacent to a busy Yosemite Valley intersection today, one tree larger and older than the others.

When Tabuce passed on in 1947, Julia wondered for a long time how she would feel if Julia used her tree. Then, one time, Julia noticed lots of acorns beneath the tree, as if she had Tabuce's permission.

Gathering from this and other trees is done in a prayerful way. "I always say, 'Well Tabuce, I think you're happy that I can pick your acorn, because I know that's what you did, and that's what I would like to do.' "

Gathering acorns off the ground, often in the company of her grandchildren, is Julia's favorite part of the process. First, she places the acorns in winnowing baskets. Then, when these are full, she uses the narrow end of the winnowing basket to funnel the acorns into a cone-shaped burden basket.

Julia treasures the connection with olden times that baskets provide. The burden basket she uses today is her second one; the original was purchased from an aunt, but has long since worn out. For her grandchildren, Julia has a smaller, tougher burden basket.

Finally, the acorn is transferred into gunnysacks. Julia cautions against substituting paper sacks for gunnysacks since the latter will break if you try to gather into them. Sometimes Julia uses boxes in the children's wagon to transport the acorn home.

Granaries outside the home of Captain Dick, a Yosemite Miwok leader, circa 1880–1890. Photographer unknown, YNPRL-14302.

Drying
And Storing

Acorns must be dried prior to storage. Julia learned the importance of proper drying soon after that first gathering trip.

Lucy gathered her acorn. Then she said, "Well, you gather some for yourself." So I gathered some for myself. . . . I had my sack of acorns. It was only half a sack. So I was going to do acorns too, so I put 'em in the sack, and I put 'em in the house. I left them there. I didn't think about it. I didn't know you have to dry them. And when I went to get my acorns, they were all molded and mildewed.

So then, next time I watched her. And she had hers out in the sun. So that's how I learned you had to dry them, see. If I had gone in and shaken the sack around and moved them around, see, 'cause the outside dried, but the inside . . . Where all the acorns were together, they didn't have a chance to dry. But the outside did. But if I'd have moved them around. So when I put them in sacks, now I do that. I move the sack around.

During the drying stage, the care taken in gathering can be fully measured. The acorns are checked from time to time and any which show insect damage (holes and bumps) are removed from the bunch and returned to the earth.

Grandmother dried her acorns on the ground atop an old quilt, old gunnysack, or old canvas cloth. Lucy gathered so many acorns that, when they were added to the acorns people always gave her, the whole hillside near her house would be covered with acorn-topped canvas.

While Grandmother never worried about the few acorns the animals might eat as they dried, Julia can no longer put hers outside lest they all be eaten by animals, who seem less afraid of humans than in years past. Instead, necessity has generated a new tradition. "I do some weird things," Julia joked about one of her innovations. Anything but weird, her new method is effective and creative.

During one particularly good year, while seeking a way to insure that no acorns would be lost to mildew, Julia came upon the idea of converting cardboard packing boxes made for twenty-four cans of soda pop into stackable drying "racks" by cutting their tops off.

Enough acorns are poured into each box to make a single layer, one acorn high. The acorns are rolled about until they completely cover the bottom of the box. Another box is stacked atop this and filled one layer high with acorns, the process being repeated until a three-foot high stack of boxes fills the corner of a room in Julia's home. Any higher and the boxes would not support the weight of the acorns. As needed, more stacks can be made. The cardboard box partitions soak up excess water. The air space between layers of acorn insures against mold.

This is but one of Julia's drying methods. Sometimes she lays her acorn in big packing cartons stacked three deep on a table. Once she spread her acorns across the floor of a room in the family's Midpines home. It was another good year for acorn, and nobody was living there at the time.

She has also put her acorns to dry in sacks or boxes beneath a clawfoot wood stove. Some ladies dry them in an oven, but Julia doesn't. If the heat is too high, the acorns can get burned or the bitterness can become baked in and never leach out.

> I found that out when . . . people would rake their yards, you know. They'd rake up the acorns, and then I'd go around and I'd . . . go to the piles and pick the acorn. And one time these acorns got burnt [after the brush pile was lit afire]. And I was picking them. And Lucy said no. Don't pick those, because those are spoilt. Because the fire has baked that bitterness in . . . I just listened to her. I figured she knew, so why should I question her. Her authority, you know.

Since "fresh" or "green" (newly gathered) acorns are too soft to shell and pound properly, acorns are usually stored for at least a year before they are used. Unshelled black oak acorns may be stored for ten to twelve years because of their high tannic acid content. Tannic acid, a natural preservative, occurs in varying amounts in acorns of different oak species.

Grandmother placed her acorns in burlap sacks for storage. Julia sometimes stores her acorns in sacks too, but she also stores them in her stackable drying racks, as well as in plastic buckets once they are dry.

First Feed

Grandmother always reserved some fresh acorn for the "first" or "big feed," the meal following each autumn's gathering. Preparing acorn for the first feed was a way of welcoming, respecting, and appreciating the new year's acorn. It was a means of letting the Creator know the people were glad for its gift. So whether acorn was plentiful or not, at least a bowlful was always gathered every year.

To hasten drying of the green acorns to be used for the feed, Lucy cracked their shells. The now partially open nuts were laid on a tarp in the sun to dry, and covered with a tarp at night. Two days to a week later, the shells were pulled off and the remaining kernels placed in the sun until completely dried and ready for winnowing. Or if the kernels were needed right away, a knife was used to cut through the shells, which were then pulled off the meats. Julia remembers sitting with Lucy on many occasions, painstakingly scraping the skin off these knife-split, green acorns before laying the nutmeats on tarps in the sun for final drying.

In addition to the first feed, green acorns were sometimes cleaned as above and cooked with acorns that had been stored for several years, since such old acorns don't thicken as well as those which are fresher.

Because shelled acorns don't preserve well, they were used soon after they dried.

Acorn Granaries[1]

Acorn storage used to occur in a granary (*chuckah*). Built off the ground above a boulder, stump, or tree round, granaries were constructed by first placing a circle of poles snugly into the ground. The poles (of pine or other saplings) ranged from six to fifteen feet long, and four or more in number. Rings of grapevine or long willow branches were wrapped around the poles in rows about one or two feet apart to form a roughly twined, open container.

The container walls were thatched with willow, deer brush, or white fir branches placed vertically inside the rings; the tip ends of these faced down toward the center of the bottom. The builder then entered the *chuckah* and began tramping down the branches, adding more and more branches to complete the walls.

Next, the interior was lined with wormwood (*Artemesia douglasiana*) and pine needles (*Pinus* spp.). The pungent, minty wormwood smell repelled insects and worms, while the pine needles kept acorns from falling through.

A helper on the ground handed the wormwood and needles to the person inside. Then the helper passed up basketfuls of dried, unshelled acorns for the builder to drop inside. As the *chuckah* filled, the builder climbed higher and higher atop the acorns until there wasn't any room for more.

Finally, the acorns were covered with more needles and wormwood, and the granary was rain- and snow-proofed with a cap of incense cedar bark, canvas, oilcloth, old blanket, or a combination of these. Animal-proofing was achieved with a shingle-style thatch of fir, cedar, or pine branches.

As needed, the acorns were removed by carefully pulling the thatch aside to form an opening, then closing the opening when the desired quantity had been emptied into a sack or basket.

Estimates indicate that such granaries could hold upwards of 500 pounds of acorns. After 1900 they became less common, as more and more people switched to the burlap sacks of Grandmother's time.

Cracking
And Shelling

Whole acorns must be cracked and shelled to release the nutmeats. As with every step, the nuances here are dictated by special methods. One by one, each acorn is held between thumb and index finger with its pointy end stabilized against a flat, rough stone. The stone provides a firm foundation for cracking, while its rough surface provides a place to secure the pointed end.

The flat end of the acorn, which was once attached to the oak tree, is then struck with the end of a small, elongated rock (hammerstone) to crack its shell. Like previous generations, Grandmother Lucy inherited her hammerstone(s) from grandmothers and mothers before her, but Julia found her own.

Julia looks for a hammerstone about one-and-a-half to two inches wide, five or more inches long, weighing about one to one-and-a-half pounds, and smoothed and rounded by the strong-flowing water of a stream; one special hammerstone with a curved handhold was found at the ocean. Julia holds the hammerstone horizontally, grasping it securely on one end with the hand that isn't holding the acorn. In cases where her hammerstone is unavailable, she finds a chunk of clean granite to use; its selection is based upon how comfortably it fits within her hand.

To crack the acorn, Julia gently taps its flat top two or three times. To protect her fingers from being smashed she lets the weight of the hammerstone do the work. She exerts only light downward pressure, so the acorn

49

Each acorn is cracked with a hammerstone.

Once cracked, the acorns are placed in another basket.

The cracked hulls are removed by hand.

kernel will be split in half or thirds, but won't be broken into a lot of small pieces.

A quiet popping sound is heard as the shell splits apart. Julia can tell if the acorn will be good just by the way it pops. "You can hear music singing," observes Julia of the steady "dum, dum, pop" of acorns being cracked.

Then the cracked hulls are removed by hand and the nutmeats inspected. Usually, whenever damage from mold, mildew, or insects is detected, the acorn is placed back with the earth from which it came; if, however, the molded or mildewed area is small, it is cut away. Mold and mildew have the appearance of green, white, or yellow fuzz, not to be confused with a natural, downy fluff on the nuts' red skins. Insect damage appears as tiny beads of the frass left when the insect excretes acorn it has consumed.

Sometimes hard, black spots are evident on the tawny nutmeats. Julia speculates that this color change happens when the acorns dry too slowly, since the spots usually appear in the center of the acorns where they would remain damp the longest. Acorns that are partially black are saved, while those that are completely blackened are returned to the earth.

Five winnowing baskets lie on the ground around Lucy Telles as she weaves a coiled basket with a three rod foundation, 1940s. Photo by Ellen St. Clair, YNPRL-16902.

Winnowing

A rusty-colored, bitter-tasting skin, some-what akin to the skin of a peanut, adheres to the acorn kernel. Great care is taken to remove even the most minute trace of skin lest, as Grandmother warned, the acorn maker be considered lazy.

Unlike some acorn species, black oak kernels have several natural grooves which enfold the skin, making it difficult to remove, so each groove must be opened up. Sometimes the cracking process splits the acorn along two or more of these grooves; the others must be split by hand. This is done by inserting the blade of a butcher or other knife into a groove longways, then exerting downward pressure.

The skins are winnowed away in a basket. Scoop-shaped, sienna and white, the basket is designed for tossing acorns into the air, thereby allowing the light, virtually weightless skins to blow away in a delicate breeze while the comparatively heavy acorns fall back into the basket. If the air is still, Julia blows on the nutmeats to simulate a breeze.

Grandmother always prepared acorn early in the morning when every-thing was quiet, cool, and calm. This is the best time to winnow and otherwise process acorn since, in quiet air, the food won't be blown to the ground. Julia can't always hold her demonstrations early in the morn-ing; however, she uses any gust of wind as an opportunity to stop and rest.

One day, I asked if the wind would be considered "destructive" to the process. Julia explained that the earth needs to be fed, too. Since acorn comes from the ground, if some falls back onto the ground that isn't harmful in and of itself; it becomes a giving back for what has been

The acorns are split along their grooves to help remove the skins.

taken. Thus, I was reminded that while working in calm weather is the best way, couching the concept in terms which imply good or bad warps its contextual meaning.

One by one, Julia rubs several handfuls of shelled acorns between her hands, and places them into the winnowing basket. As they're rubbed, they abrade against each other, causing the skins to loosen.

Once in the basket, the acorns are sometimes further rubbed, this time against each other and the basket's weave. When she is doing the latter, Julia supports the basket from below with the palm of one hand if she is standing, or holds it in her lap if she is sitting. She rubs the acorns back and forth along the basket with the other hand, which exerts a downward pressure. From time to time, the basket is also shaken back and forth to help loosen the skins.

Next, while standing, Julia deftly moves the basket so the nutmeats are tossed repeatedly into the air. Here the skill of the acorn maker comes to the fore, as the acorns gently rise a few inches above the basket, then fall back into its cradling concavity. While they rise, a shower of tiny red skin-flecks take wing, floating delicately in the air. As the acorns fall back into the basket, other skins ease through spaces between the basket's

Julia rubs handfuls of shelled acorns between her hands to loosen the skins.

weave, filling the air below and slowly making their way to the earth.

All the while, the basket seems to glide of its own accord, but in fact Julia is its guide. Her motion is barely perceptible, smooth, fluid, effortless. Like anyone with a skill honed to perfection, she makes it seem easy, although this is far from reality.

The acorns are further rubbed against each other in the basket's weave.

"I go way up highhhh with the big one."

While tossing the nutmeats, Julia grips the basket end-to-end between her hands, thumbs above, fingers below. She holds the basket level to the ground, with her upper arms at her side and her elbows bent so her lower arms extend forward, parallel to the ground.

The basket is moved by raising her lower arms up and down, bending at her elbows (her wrists rigid, yet relaxed). Starting with the basket at waist height, it is gradually brought higher and higher, always level with the ground until it is up to chest, shoulder, or head height. As she brings the basket higher, Julia raises her upper arms, transferring the motion from her elbows to her upper arms, which are extended forward more and more as the basket is lifted.

How high the basket is raised depends in part upon its size. The larger the basket, the higher it can go without spillage: "I go way up highhhhh with the big one. It's fun to do." First-time winnowers learn by hardly lifting the basket at all and, when Julia first starts a day's winnowing, she reconditions herself to the motions by not bringing the basket too high at first.

The higher Julia brings the basket, the more effectively the movement carries away the skins. Every so often, Julia stops winnowing to inspect the acorns. Those without the slightest trace of skin are picked out and set aside, each a silken, shiny, tawny yellow. As needed, more shelled acorn is added to the basket. Julia rubs the acorns together as before in preparation for another series of tosses.

Winnowing replaces the tedious knife-scraping used to remove green acorn skin, a process which is time-consuming and unnecessary when working with acorn that has been dried and stored. Other than green acorn for the "first feed" and to mix with old acorn, the only time Julia scrapes by hand is to clean the occasional wrinkly nutmeat, which catches the skin in its furrows so forcefully that winnowing is ineffective.

As winnowing progresses, nutmeats with recalcitrant skins are quickly spread in a single layer across a tarp or blanket without regard to whether the round or flat sides face up, which would slow the process; sprinkled with water flicked from fingertips; then sun-dried. From time to time, they are moved around to speed evaporation, which ultimately shrinks and loosens the skins. Once they are completely dried, the acorns are winnowed anew.

Any acorns that still have traces of skin after winnowing are stored in a paper bag (Grandmother used a flour sack) and saved until the next time Julia winnows. By this time, their skins will have loosened further.

"You've got to be friends with the rock."
— *Julia F. Parker*

Pounding

After winnowing, the cleaned kernels are pounded between pestle and mortar. Like acorn trees, the mortars are owned by an individual or family, each one handed down through the generations; every woman has her own special rock.

In the Indian Village, Lucy Telles was well known for her proficiency at pounding. Such was Lucy's dedication to providing acorn that she pounded acorn anytime, even in the rain. To keep the small mortar outside her home dry, a tarp supported by poles was stretched across.

Rather than carry her pestles to the pounding area for each use, Grandmother buried them nearby, uncovering and cleaning them as needed. The only thing she kept with her was the oak burl mortar, made by her father, that she inherited from her mother. It was about 14 inches deep, varied from about 18 to 24 inches wide, and had a tapered bowl about 13 inches wide at its rim and 6 inches wide at its base. Visible inside this approximately 50-pound mortar was a pretty, wrinkly wood grain.

Other women pounded in the Village, but less frequently than Grandmother. After Lucy passed on, her sister Alice Wilson, who subsequently inherited their father's burl mortar, was responsible for the acorn. Usually Alice and Julia, who helped her pound, used the burl mortar. Alice preferred it for sentimental and logistical reasons. Although there were bedrock mortars to use, they were inconvenient to Alice's home. Acorns, baskets, and other supplies would have to be hauled to them. One such bedrock was up a hill; the other near another family's home.

Sometimes Alice and Julia used the large, flat bedrock where all the ladies had pounded with Lucy, but the burl mortar, which was placed beneath a tree or at another cool area near Alice's home, remained the preferred choice. As heavy as it was, Julia and Alice would drag it, roll it, or have the men carry it to the desired locale.

After Alice passed on, the burl mortar was given to her relatives on the East Side of the Sierra. Julia, who hasn't seen the burl since, went on to pound for Phoebe Hogan, who was fluent in her Southern Miwok language. Phoebe considered herself "as kind of a captain," and said she could never pound acorn. Instead, she used to shell and clean the acorns, then direct Julia to pound, bringing her lunch while she worked. Julia, who pounded alone for Phoebe, chose a bedrock mortar less isolated than the one she had previously used with other women.

These years of training and experience have given Julia a proficiency which is astounding to watch. As she works, the pestle rises and falls, seemingly without effort, belying its weight.

The enjoyment Julia brings to her task is evident. One supposes she could continue unceasingly but, in a mere fifteen minutes or so, she has pounded enough for a batch of acorn: "And we used to just get lots of flour. It's amazing how fast."

Strength gained by lifting and re-lifting pestles over countless hours serves Julia in many ways. One evening in May of 1990, she rolled out about 45 pounds of white wheat flour dough to make Indian frybread for a community gathering without experiencing any soreness. And in June of the same year she joined several Miwok/Paiute people on an historic, 47-mile hike across ancestral trading trails from the east side of the Sierra, over the rugged 11,000-foot Mono Pass, and into Yosemite Valley.

When she isn't publicly demonstrating acorn making, Julia pounds on a rock close to her family's government house, a short walk west of the Yosemite Valley visitor center. Since no suitable rock was already there, in about 1986 Julia searched out a flat piece of granite less than a foot high and about three feet wide. Instead of chipping out a mortar depression, Julia sets her acorn right on top of the more or less flat rock. While it's easier if there's a shallow depression, Julia finds it will work if the crushed acorn is re-piled often enough.

For public demonstrations, Julia uses a bedrock mortar which is flat and comfortable to sit atop. It sits behind the visitor center in the "Indian Garden" where Lucy once demonstrated on her own and where Julia herself now demonstrates as part of her job. The rock was moved to its

Before pounding, Julia cleans a one-hand pestle with her pitch-handled soaproot brush.

present location from elsewhere in Yosemite Valley. Now it sits low to the ground, most of it buried, amid a cultural exhibit of *umuchas* and other structures built by Park Service employees.

Such a pounding rock would usually be off to one side, but it was placed in a central area so park visitors could watch the pounding from every direction. As Julia pounds, a crowd invariably appears.

The visitors' movements can cause dust to fly. Julia doesn't want dust to contaminate the food, so to keep it down she places incense cedar boughs and pine needles on the ground around the mortar. After the alder tree that used to shade the mortar fell, Julia put a brush sunshade over the rock, which was later rebuilt by other employees. She has woven small branches around its poles. The rounded sunshade serves several purposes — it makes the rock a comfortable working area, keeps people back from the mortar during pounding and serves as a protective barrier at other times.

Unlike Julia, Lucy never needed a sunshade. The Indian Village was a shady place, and Lucy worked early in the morning. In desert areas, however, such a sunshade was essential.

Julia remembers a Paiute shade shelter that Rosie August, one of her basketry teachers, used to shade her pounding rock, which was in the desert near Bridgeport. The rock was heavy; it had taken four men to lift it into place. When Rosie took Julia to see it, a big, rounded pile of sagebrush was the only thing there. Rosie moved a hidden "door" in the sagebrush, however, to reveal the stone secure inside what turned out to be a "little, sagebrush house" supported on a frame of what may have been willow poles.

Grandmother was immaculate with her acorn. Because it was food, Lucy treated her nuts and acorn flour carefully; she made sure no dust and dirt got into them. The natural layer of fallen pine needles and oak leaves which covered the Indian Village grounds, and the fact that Lucy usually worked alone or with only a few others, kept the areas around her rocks dust-free.

Additionally, Lucy would not allow children around when she pounded acorn. Their place was solely to help gather and eat.

> *That's all. Because their little hands are no way going to do these things. You know what you have to do. Winnow and crack it, open and then pound it. There's some, but most of the kids play with the stuff. And you don't put your hands and*

play in that flour in the basket, which kids will kind of want to do. To me, it's too valuable and too sacred to use it for play.

Ultimately, food preparation was a privilege that was earned, starting, as always, with learning by observation long before the doing. If children are nearby when Julia pounds, she involves them with guarding the acorn, assigning them to special duties, like making sure the Stellar's jays or the squirrels don't chase after the food. In so doing, she instills caring while protecting the food.

The bedrock mortar holes in which Julia pounds are shallow, usually less than a half inch in depth. Deeper holes are used to pound acorn in many areas, but the flour that results from pounding the comparatively oily black oak acorn will build up in the bottom of deep holes like peanut butter, making pounding ineffective.

Over long use, food residue will coat the inside of a mortar hole; its smooth sheen protects the hole from the elements. Removal of the residue requires vigorous scrubbing, so different bedrock mortars are usually reserved for different foods.

For instance, Julia has a somewhat deeper mortar which she usually reserves for crushing ripe, red manzanita (*Arctostaphylos viscida*) berries. A sweet, refreshing cider is made from sugars which form in the berries' inner skins as they ripen.

Once, Julia saw Lucy make manzanita cider by letting crushed berries sit in a gallon jar of cold water. The sweetness seeped from the berry skins into the water, which became the cider, then Lucy transferred the liquid into a clean container. The heavier berry skins and seeds, which had settled to the bottom of the jar, were left behind.

Although Julia never saw the ladies clean manzanita berries, she has innovated her own method to remove dust from their naturally sticky skin. First, the berries are placed in a loosely woven winnowing basket, then rinsed. When working near a faucet, she lets the water run over them. Otherwise, she rinses them with water flicked from fingertips.

Next, the berries are rubbed gently back and forth against the winnowing basket until the tiny, adhering sticks come loose, then rinsed anew so the sticks are washed through the basket's weave. The berries are transferred into a 2-quart cooking basket until nearly dry, then lightly crushed between mortar and pestle, leaving their hard, black seeds intact.

The mashed berries and their seeds are next placed atop a porous but

When no starter is available, the whole, winnowed acorns are crushed with several light downward hits of the pestle. This mortar is deeper than those Julia usually uses to crush acorn.

After the acorns are mashed between mortar and pestle, another handful of whole nutmeats will be added.

After being pounded for a while longer, the acorn meal will be ready to sift.

closely woven sifting basket. To wash (leach) out the sweetness, cold water is poured through the crushed berries. The liquid seeps through the basket's weave, which contains the berries' skins and seeds. It drips into a cooking basket, then is re-poured through the berries as many times as it takes to attain the desired sweetness, gradually turning the water deeper and deeper shades of red.

Julia uses about one-and-a-half cups of cold water for each cup of berries she leaches. She can tell if the cider will be flavorful enough by the water's color; too deep a shade of red means the cider is so sweet that water must be added to lighten the flavor.

When pounding acorn, many groups of California Indians who used it placed a bottomless "hopper basket" around their mortar holes to contain the acorn. However, other groups, including the Miwok/Paiute people of Yosemite, didn't. Julia thinks this may be because black oak acorns don't bounce around as much as other acorn species during pounding.

> I've always wondered why the Yosemite ladies never had a hopper. I never knew what a hopper was until I saw the Pomos using that [in a movie]. And I was wondering why would they have that and us not have it up here. Then I thought more about it. It's the texture of the acorn. This acorn here is more oilier and more softer. And yet, it's hard, but when you pound it, it's gonna crush up easier.

Before starting to pound, the mortar is cleaned with several sweepings of a soaproot brush. Sometimes the mortar is swept when dry, but other times, if its dirt is hard to remove, Julia pours water over it prior to sweeping. Then she lets it thoroughly dry before proceeding with her task.

Julia is saddened that people who see untended bedrock mortars often don't know or respect their purpose. All manner of dirt, acorn husk, and rock fragments are picked off the ground and left on the mortar rock, necessitating a more thorough cleaning than if natural processes alone were responsible.

Once the rock is cleaned, and before adding any acorn, Julia usually sits with legs outstretched, knees unbent, around the mortar depression. When demonstrating, she sometimes wears the type of long, late 1800s-style dress the ladies once wore, and must carefully tuck the skirt out of the way. Recently, she has also begun to sit on the side of the bedrock

The relatively light blows used at this stage keep the nutmeats from hopping around. Here, Julia is using a small "two-hand rock."

with her feet on the ground when using only one hand to hold the pestle, finding this to be easier.

Unless she has been pounding frequently, Julia starts gradually, working her way up to heavier pestles and an increasingly larger pile of acorn. The larger pestles, which take two hands to handle, can cause back or arm strain, so it's important to be in shape before attempting to use them.

> *I'm not going to start with that big old [12 pound] rock. No.*
> *Because I've got to think about my arms. It's just like you*
> *overwork your arms. Your muscles are going to tighten up, and*
> *you're going to get sore. So you start a little at a time . . . and*
> *rest, and do some more.*

As she was taught, Julia starts beginners with a three- to four-pound pestle she calls a "one-hand rock," because of how it's used, then graduates them to a medium sized rock. Then she tells them with a laugh, "If you want to be Jayne Mansfield, tackle the bigger one."

Even the one-hand rock is heavy to use, "Like I tell the women," Julia explains, "We don't need Jack LaLanne exercise or stretching or stuff like that, because the Indians were getting it all the time by stretching out on that rock. And [the back of] your legs are stretched right out."

Just as Lucy inherited her pestles, Julia sometimes pounds with pestles that once belonged to Lucy; after Lucy died, Julia had asked Ralph if she could keep them. In addition to Lucy's pestles, Julia also chooses her own stout pestles from a stream bed. Each of Julia's pestles has an ever so slightly rough surface so it won't slip in her hands. Ranging from six-and-one-half, eight-and-one-half, ten-and-one-half, to twelve inches long, Julia's favorite pestles are four, five, ten, and fourteen pounds respectively. The heavier the pestle, the quicker the flour forms.

Beginners need about six handfuls of whole, freshly winnowed nuts to start. A palm-sized, one-hand pestle is balanced upright in the mortar depression (even a slight, natural depression on a bedrock will do) so it stands by itself, then one handful of nuts placed around it. Grasped in the right hand, the pestle is lifted, causing the nuts to fall into the depression. They're now in place to be crushed with several light, downward blows of the pestle.

These light blows are designed to prevent the nuts from bouncing around on the mortar. Once mashed, another handful of nuts is added and gently crushed using the same technique, although this time the pestle is balanced inside a small, bowl-shaped pile of crushed nutmeats.

The process is repeated until four handfuls of winnowed nuts are well crushed. If at any time along the way the right hand tires, the pestle can be switched to the left.

Holding the pestle above the meal, another handful of whole nuts is added, this time into the bottom of the bowl, and crushed. The previously crushed acorn keeps the fresh nuts from bouncing around, so heavier blows are used at this stage. Once these new nuts are crushed, the sixth and final handful is added. After this pile has been pounded a few more minutes, the acorn is ready to be sifted. About half a cupful of usable flour, along with about a cupful of leftover, partially-pounded acorn, results from sifting. The latter, called "starter acorn," is reserved for the next pounding day.

Experienced pounders like Julia, who always have a batch of leftover starter, use a somewhat different method. Julia generally begins by standing a five- to eight-pound "two-hand rock" upright in the mortar depression. After saying "a little prayer" of thanks for the acorn and hoping to do a good job, she reaches for a handful of starter. If it is used almost every day, Julia stores the starter on a shelf in a quart jar or cloth bag; otherwise, it's stored in a plastic bag in the refrigerator. Grandmother stored hers in a cool place inside a muslin, flour, or sugar sack.

Several handfuls of starter, at least three or four, are spread around the balanced pestle — enough that a cushion of acorn will fall into the mortar when Julia grasps the pestle between her hands and lifts it above the mortar. There isn't a set amount of starter or whole nuts to use; the goal of each pounding day is to use up all the previous day's starter, no matter how much or how little, since starter will get oily sitting around.

Ideally, at least one-and-a-half inches of acorn should cover the mortar. If the cushion looks to be only about half an inch or so deep, the pestle is once more balanced upright, this time atop whatever acorn has fallen into the depression, and another handful of starter is added around it before any blows are struck. This prevents the pestle from striking directly against the mortar during pounding.

Once starter is in place, a few light blows are struck with the pestle firmly grasped between both hands. The pestle is re-balanced in the meal, and a handful (or two if the acorns are small) of whole, winnowed acorn added around it. Starter keeps the whole nutmeats from bouncing around during pounding. The addition of whole kernels keeps the flour from getting pasty, a quality which results from the acorns' natural oils coming out when repeatedly crushed.

Whole kernels absorb the oil, preventing stickiness. This is of particular concern with cold, refrigerated starter, which has a lot of oil and doesn't separate easily during pounding. If it is too sticky, the acorn flour will form little, beaded clumps during sifting, and it will not dissolve in water at leaching time.

Once starter and whole kernels are in place, the pestle is lifted about two inches above the rock surface. A downward blow is made, with the pestle firmly grasped all the while. The relatively soft blows used at this stage are designed to mash the whole nutmeats and keep them from hopping around.

As pounding progresses, and the whole kernels begin to break up, the pestle is once more balanced in the meal and another handful of starter or whole nuts is added. This is hit a little bit more, then a pause taken while the pestle is re-balanced in the growing pile of acorn, and another handful of clean, whole kernels added. If more than a handful was added at a time, the acorn would jump all over.

After four to six handfuls of whole kernels are added and crushed in the same way (alternating with starter if any remains), a volcano-shaped pile at least two inches high is formed, and the starter and newly added kernels are mixed and crushed. Then pounding begins in earnest.

> *I just pound the heck out of it. That's what I do. I pound it and*
> *pound it. I don't worry about pounding it too much.*

The pestle is gradually lifted higher, to chest, shoulder, head, or even higher height, crushing the acorn further. As in the earlier stages of two-hand rock use, the hands grasp the pestle firmly from both sides as they lift it. Unlike the earlier stages, they're relaxed around the pestle as it descends, serving merely to guide the pestle toward the mortar during these longer downward blows; gravity and the weight of the rock do the work.

As she works, Julia's body sways, moving back as she lifts the pestle, and forward as it descends. This swaying is from her hips. Her back is kept straight; if it begins to ache, she knows to straighten it. Anytime she needs a break, Julia leaves her pestle standing in the mound of meal. The meal supports it upright, leaving it in position for being lifted anew, which in turn allows the unpounded pieces to fall back inside the volcano.

With each blow of the pestle, the rock vibration causes pieces of coarse, partially pounded acorn to mound around the pestle. As the pestle is lifted, these fall back down into the hole, ready to be reduced to a finer

Rebuilding the pile, using a soaproot brush.

consistency by the weight of the pestle. At the same time, any blackened pieces of acorn slide out of the mortar and away from the flour since they are too hard for the pestle to crush.

Julia takes pride in the neat, fluffy mound of acorn which forms during pounding. The natural oils in the acorns serve to moisturize and soften the hands, while the occasional addition of whole kernels helps keep the meal fluffy.

It's time to rebuild the pile if the meal layer on the inside of the mortar depression becomes too thin. When this happens, the mortar and pestle "talk" (change tones). As a thick layer (about 1-1/2 inches) of acorn between mortar and pestle becomes thinner (about 1/2 inch) in the mortar, the thud of pounding becomes more ringing. Even burl mortars, which produce a lower tone to begin with, will change sounds although the change is less detectable than with rock.

To rebuild the pile, the pestle is again balanced in the meal. Then any acorn meal which has fallen beyond the mound of meal and onto the bedrock is swept up against the side of the pestle with a soaproot brush, ready to fall into the mortar when the pestle is lifted. As with winnowing, any acorn that falls on the ground is left to feed the earth.

When she is warmed up, Julia switches to a larger pestle, a two-hand rock which weighs on the order of nine, ten, sometimes fourteen pounds, to speed flour formation. The switch can occur at any time once the acorn is pretty well broken up and the pile covers a good portion of the rock.

Grasped between both hands, this larger pestle is lifted to shoulder, head or even higher height as well, then guided toward the mortar. When Julia pounds every day, she's able to lift it higher.

By proceeding with a steady, relaxed rhythm, it's possible to pound for a long time without getting tired. Just let the pestle fall and pick it up, then let it fall again. As with scraping willow or cracking acorns, Julia maintains a steady rhythm during pounding. She pounds until the rock "sings" to her with a steady thud-ding and thud-ding reminiscent of a drum.

Julia starts to sing songs from a still popular adult Indian gambling game called Handgame when she "really gets going." "Like Superwoman!" she quips. All the while, the pestle repeats its "dun dun dun" as Julia moves back and forth, back and forth, until it's time to rest. Depending on how much flour is desired, Julia can keep pounding the same acorn until it's ready to sift, or increase the amount by adding and crushing a handful of whole kernels from time to time.

Whole kernels can keep the pile growing to six inches high and covering half the bedrock, so long as there is room to grasp the pestle between the hands. Although Julia likes to work with a lot of acorn, she doesn't usually have the time to get that much done. When Julia and Lucy pounded, however, they made huge piles of acorn around their pestles. As Julia once exclaimed about Lucy, "Oh, yeah! She just used to have that acorn pile high!"

The flour is ready to sift when acorn pieces no longer fall into the bottom of the mound as the pestle is lifted and the flour sticks to the hand.

Stereotypes Dispelled

Two pervasive but incorrect assumptions about acorn processing are dispelled by Julia. First, there is the notion that acorn flour is created by "grinding." Julia is quick to remind people that no such rubbing action is used; the process is strictly one of pounding or hitting and crushing the acorns.

The second idea is related to the first — that stone grit wears off the mortar from pounding, getting into the meal. Indeed, if granite hits granite the rocks can crack. However, throughout the entire pounding process, Julia is fastidious about preventing such rock-on-rock contact. She always maintains a layer of meal at least one-half inch thick between mortar and pestle, completely guarding against rock wear.

While Julia is uncertain how the holes in bedrock mortars were made, she has heard that some of the ladies started holes by hitting the granite with a harder rock. Evidence that the holes were purposefully created to the desired depth before ever being used has been found in several places.

The late Rosa Bill (Dry Creek Pomo) is known to have made a portable mortar in the 1950s by chipping it with an axe head.[1] Western Mono consultants recalled seeing bedrock mortar holes of the desired size made with "star bits" earlier in this century.[2] And, when Maggie Marvin (Western Mono) needed a mortar close to home, she made one using a hammerstone and metal bar.[3]

As for the varied depths of mortar holes, these seem to have depended on what was pounded in them and local preference. Seeds, berries, mineral paints, and other things were pounded or crushed in their own mortars. Among the Western Mono, mortar depth depended on type of use: mortars used to start pounding acorn are the shallowest; seed pounding mortars are the deepest; and acorn finishing mortars are in between.[4]

This soaproot brush, made by Ida Bishop, was a gift to Julia. Photo by Raye Santos, 1990.

Soaproot Brushes

About 30 years ago, Julia received something she would always treasure—a soaproot brush from the late Ida Bishop (Northfork Mono).

The brush is lovely to behold, wonderful in its smooth, clean, white handle, and the vibrant reddish browns of its tough, resilient fiber. It is treasured because it was made by Ida, and made dearer by the years Julia has used it to sweep her sifting basket and the acorn on her pounding stone.

Such brushes are made almost entirely from the bulb of a lily (*Chloragalum pertidinum*). Soaproot is recognizable by its curly, long and slender, shiny green leaves, which creep along the ground surface in all directions from its base. At times one sees a tall stalk, perhaps two or three feet in length, capped with small branchlets. At the end of each branchlet a tiny, delicate, white flower clings, closed by day, open by evening.

Soaproot gets its name from its soapy bulb, which is protected within the earth by a thick covering of fibers. It is a multi-purpose bulb. When stripped of its fibers, it can be used as a bar of soap; as such it gets the hands "squeaky clean," but leaves no residue and doesn't dry the skin.

Its starchy, inner core can also be crushed and sudsed into water pooling in a river to clog fishes' gills and kill them. So effective is this aeons-old fishing technique that it is now against the law. The inner core of soaproot can also be boiled, then rubbed against a fairly loosely woven basket to extract a gluey pulp. Upon hardening, this pulp, used to coat some gathering baskets, keeps even the tiniest of seeds from falling through the basket's weave.

In fashioning a soaproot brush, the first steps are to know where the plant comes from and when to gather it, and to say a little prayer of thanks or make a little ceremony or offering when gathering. Soaproot is dug in the late spring. The digging tool of olden times was a long, straight stick of mountain mahogany or buckbrush (chaparral), stripped of its bark, with one pointed, fire-hardened end.

The ease with which soaproot can be dug depends on the soil in the area where it's sought. As with other bulbs, the digging loosens and aerates the soil, spreading offsets, and making it more plentiful and easier to dig in subsequent years.

In Julia's area, the ground is damp, but it is also rocky and a little bit hard to dig.

> By using a digging stick it helps you to get into the earth. And then when you get going you can use your own two hands, which are your first digging tools. And so you can pull away the dirt.
>
> And I remember this one time that I was digging the soaproot. I kept digging and digging, and I was wondering if I was doing it wrong, because I could never get down to the bottom of the soaproot. And I kept digging and digging, and pulling and digging and pulling, and it took me almost 40, 30 minutes to pull and dig this soapbulb. And I'd sit there and yank on it, you know. And it wouldn't come out. Finally, I just kept digging and digging, using my stick and my fingers and my hands.
>
> I don't know if any of you have ever gone out and sat. Maybe when you were little you remember doing this — sitting in there and playing in the dirt — and your parents or mother would say, "That's dirty." But when I think about this, you know, that that earth is clean and that earth is special. And so sometime maybe you might want to try it. Sit there and feel the coolness of the earth.
>
> So after digging, I finally was able to pull the soapbulb out. And I was lucky because 4 bulbs were growing together and they were about as big as my fist. Four of them were sitting together. So see I was like the person who thought maybe it wouldn't be there, but then again it was there for me to find it like that.

Julia sometimes cleans soaproot fibers by dry-combing them with an awl made from a deer cannon bone.

After getting the four soapbulbs, Julia was anxious to take them home and make them into brushes. (Depending on the size of the brush to be made, several bulbs may be needed.) Remembering Ida Bishop, Julia had a goal, although she had never been taught to make a soaproot brush.

> *I had a good friend who gave me a soaproot brush, and I always wanted to make a soaproot brush just like hers. I took the fibers off of it first, [combed them with a bone awl] . . . and boiled the bulb, and made the brush. But my brush [handle] didn't look like hers. It wasn't a nice, white color. So I was thinking maybe it was because I had boiled the bulb, and it had some dirt in it, and when the soap came out, it was kind of dirty looking. So I thought, well I'm going to try and find another way to make the soapbulb clean. So I thought why not boil it just like you boil a potato with the skin on.*

Originally, Julia had dry combed the fibers after pulling them away from the bulb, but dry combing created enough dust to make her sneeze, so she developed the idea of boiling the bulb with the fibers still attached.

First, she beats the bulb against a rock to remove excess dust and dirt from its fibers, then she boils it in a pot for about 30 minutes, loosening dirt from the fibers.

Once, as an experiment, Julia tried baking a bulb like a potato in her oven at 350 degrees for about 30 or 45 minutes. She found it to be pasty, sticky, and to have hardly any water compared to a boiled bulb. Consequently, unless water was added to the baked bulb, it was harder to work with.

After the hot, boiled bulb cools, it is easy to pull the outer fibers free from the now gluey inner bulb. The fibers grow with a natural curve, following the line of the bulb, so that only their skyward end is straight. With the straight ends grasped firmly in one hand, Julia dips the fibers into a ponded creek, then scrubs them vigorously back and forth against a flat, granitic rock embedded on the edge of the creek. As an alternative to the rock ("You're going to laugh at me," said Julia), the fibers are scrubbed against a washboard sitting in a water-filled, cast-iron pot.

The water creates a sudsy soap from the bulb residue that adheres to the fibers, readily cleansing them of dust and dirt. Then they're combed with a bone awl, scrubbed, combed, scrubbed and combed until every strand is clean.

"That stuff is strong!" Julia says about the fibers. Indeed, the strength of the fibers is remarkable, and only the weakest fibers, which are greyish in color, and the shortest fibers are washed away during the scrubbing procedure. These fibers would have broken if they were bound into the finished brush. The good, strong fibers stick together and are the underpinning of a durable brush.

Once thoroughly scrubbed, the fiber bundles are neatly laid out to dry in a cardboard box. Then Julia takes the needed amount of fiber in her hand and lines all the curved and straight ends neatly together. She wraps the straight ends round and round with string to the desired handle length and then trims away any excess fiber.

Julia likes to make her string by hand from dogbane (*Apocynum* spp., "Indian hemp"). As with soaproot, the first steps are to know where the hemp comes from, and when to gather it, and to say a little prayer of thanks, or make a ceremony or offering.

Dogbane fibers were used to make string and rope by many groups of California Indians. The three- to four-foot stalks are gathered in the fall, after the first frosts have caused the leaves to yellow, die, and fall from the plant, and the sap to "drop" into the rootbase, but before the stalk

To make the handle, the soaproot fibers are wrapped round and round with dogbane string.

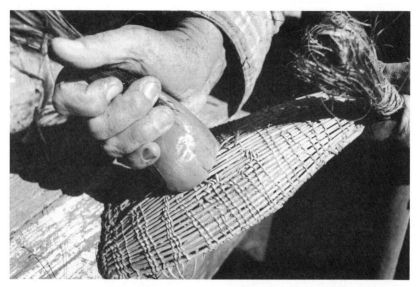

The pulp is removed by rubbing the bulb against the back of a basket that Julia made especially for this purpose. The bundle of fibers in her left hand will also be rubbed to remove the pulp from bulb material which has adhered to them.

has been weathered so long it begins to deteriorate, changing from a red to greyish hue, and becoming frayed. The rootbase stays alive through winter, until spring's rejuvenation sends up another stalk.

The dead stalk, with its vivid red-brown fibers, is cut both below any side branches, and at the base, leaving a straight stalk free of buds. While the cut tip is offered back to the environment with a thank you, the now straight stalks are bundled and tied with cord or rag, with the growing ends all facing the same way. These are stored for later string making.

As she does with all the natural materials she works with, Julia approaches this plant with a thoughtful reverence for its growing rhythm. She has designated the growing or upper end "the sky end;" the opposite side "the earth end."

Julia has developed her own method to extract the fiber, which lies in a thin strip beneath a tissue-thin, papery, skin-like layer of bark and above a woody core. The bark is gently scraped off the fibers from earth to sky end — in the same direction people and plants grow — with a butcher knife or sharpened piece of obsidian. Care is taken not to scrape

Paste from the soaproot bulb will be used for the handle.

so hard the fibers are cut and broken. Instead, a little bit of skin is left to hold the fibers together.

To remove the woody core, Julia sometimes cracks the stem-base in her teeth, then grasps the stalk at this point, running her fingertips firmly up its length. Other times, in deference to her dentist, she lightly crushes the stalk with a stone. This breaks the stalk into four sections. Julia runs her finger through the middle of the sections, dividing the stalk in half. Then she runs her finger along each half, flattening it. Finally, the two halves are laid side by side.

Starting an inch or two up from the earth end, section after section of the woody stalk is broken and pulled away from the fibers, until only fibers remain in one continuous hair-like strand. Grasping the strand of fibers at the earth end, Julia runs fingertips dipped in water along and through them to loosen any remaining skin and smooth the fiber.

Then the strand is combed with a bone awl or sharpened stick pulled again and again from earth to sky end, until the fibers are separated from each other, the fiber strand is fluffy, and all bark is gone. The earth end is thicker (has more fibers) than the sky end. Thinking about how to insure an even fiber strand, Julia has begun to grasp the strand with both hands, one at the earth-, the other at the sky-end, and shake it. This exposes the ends of any shorter fibers, which Julia picks out and makes into a separate pile for later use, sometimes balling them up.

Then Julia pulls enough fibers from the strand to make a string of the desired diameter. These are doubled over. Starting at the bend, Julia continuously twists and rolls the fibers between her fingers, taking first one half, then the other half, until a sturdy two-ply string is made. As needed to increase its length, new fibers are spliced to the old.

Any discarded stalk and scrapings are left on the ground to return to the earth. When working inside the museum, Julia gathers these leavings onto a cloth, takes them outside, shakes them out beneath a tree, and says thank you. "If you want to learn Indian ways, you do that," Julia instructs.

Lucy Telles taught Julia to recycle the leavings. Once, when Lucy was sitting at her place on a certain rock behind her home scraping willows to size for a basket, Julia picked up the scrapings. There was a firepit nearby, and Julia thought she'd be helpful and burn them in the fire.

But Lucy admonished, "No, Julia. We don't burn it up. We just throw it away." Later, when Julia was thinking about what Lucy said, she thought the reason might be that when burned it was like the end. It wouldn't grow anymore. It was gone forever. But when spread over the soil, it was like still being alive. It would feed the soil and grow again.

The brush handle is coated with a pasty pulp extracted from the boiled or baked bulb or bulbs, depending on the brush's size. The bulb, stripped of its fibers, is rubbed against the back (convex) side of a winnowing or other open twined basket until its pulp squeezes through the somewhat loose weave of the basket. Julia also uses a stainless steel collander turned upside down in her kitchen sink to rub the pulp from the bulb. She also recommends a sieve or screen as an alternative.

The bulbs are rubbed until virtually all the pulp is extracted and some tiny, yellow, especially stiff and tough fibers are revealed. Honoring the adage, "Waste not, want not," Julia washes these strong, light-colored fibers, which are mixed together every which way, then lines them up to make miniature brushes, sometimes less than a half inch long.

When Julia wishes to be especially careful of these fibers, she peels off the bulb layers one at a time and rubs out all the pulp, setting aside the fibers once they are nice and clean. The process is repeated until all pulp is extracted and all fibers cleaned.

Whichever fibers are used, a thin layer of pulp is spread over the brush

*The brush handle is coated with the first of several layers
of pulp.*

handle, then allowed to dry thoroughly. This is followed by five or six other thin coatings in as many days, much like a person would varnish a table. With each successive day and coating, the handle bristles disappear into the increasingly opaque handle coating.

This process brings a vibrant reminder of that old lesson that these things should not, indeed cannot be hurried. If one layer is not allowed to dry before the next is applied, or if the layers are placed too thickly, the completed handle will crack. Patience. It is a hard and uncomfortable lesson for those who live their lives in a rush.

Once the last layer is in place, Julia dips her hand in water, then rolls it around the handle to form the desired shape. When dry, the completed handle is smooth, thick, and of a dull white or slightly tan color. Each of the brushes, like the plants they come from, is different, individual. Julia is observant of these differences.

One time, when she was demonstrating soaproot brush-making in Mariposa, where it is hotter than Yosemite and each layer dries faster, Julia noticed the handle got shinier. Variations in fiber color also occur. In some brushes the bristles have a dark, reddish hue, while in others they are different shades of brown. Julia attributes this to variations in the food within the earth that's available to each plant.

Brushes are strong, able to stand up to hard, rough work. Each brush is kept for its own individual use. They are sometimes used like a whisk broom to clean baskets and pounding rocks of acorn flour, sometimes used to brush hair, or even, as Julia sometimes does, to sweep carpets. Unlike contemporary brushes, it's the curly side, rather than the flatter side, which brushes against the surface to be cleaned.

If the brush handles get wet, they will soften and start to disintegrate. When needed, a water-resistant handle is made out of heated pitch and charcoal. To make such a handle, the first step is, as always, to locate the materials, gather, and give thanks.

Pitch is a sticky resin that oozes from wounds in pine trees during the summertime, sealing the injury so disease organisms can't enter. The time to gather is after cold weather, which causes pitch to solidify, has settled in.

In such a solidified state pitch can be stored indefinitely. Then, as needed, it is combined with charcoal dust (experience dictates how much is necessary for the handle to ultimately harden). First the pitch is heated in a coffee can until it boils, then the heat is lowered and the charcoal is added. To make the dust, Julia takes a chunk of charcoal from a firepit, then grates it with a small, metal cheese grater or rubs it with her fingers. Julia dips the fiber handle of the brush into the melted pitch and charcoal mixture rather than coating it with soaproot. The pitch begins to harden immediately. While it's cool to touch, but still slightly soft, she shapes the handle by hand.

Holding the pitched handle of a soaproot brush, Julia taps it with her fingernail. A low, ringing sound is heard. "Indian fiberglass," she announces.

Sifting

Pounded meal is sifted to insure its even-
ness. As Julia explains, "You don't want
to have coarse and fine. You want to have
fine flour. That's the right way to make it.
That's how I was taught to make it. Real fine. So fine it just blows away
with the wind."

Good sifting requires an utterly amazing, finely tuned degree of skill.
This is not the kind of sifting most people are familiar with. The object
here is to keep the finest flour in the sifting basket rather than let it
escape through a screen.

Grandmother always did the sifting. "We couldn't sift. We didn't know
how," Julia says. "She knew." After a woman had pounded for a while,
Grandmother came by with the sifting basket, providing her with a
well-deserved rest. Such was Grandmother's ability that she could not
only tell if the acorn was ready to sift just by looking at it, but she was
also able to sift about four handfuls of flour at a time; the more flour
used, the larger the sifting basket.

Before sifting, Lucy scooped all the acorn in the mortar hole off to
one side. As Julia recalls, Lucy was so "perfect" with her sifting technique
all the coarse particles that needed re-pounding would end up in a single
pile back in the same mortar hole in front of her.

When Grandmother died, Julia had never sifted acorn. Instead, she
turned to memory for inspiration. While many of the Yosemite people
used the circular sifting baskets of the Miwok, Julia learned on the Paiute
and Western Mono type of sifting basket, which is less rounded, at times

Julia usually starts by placing three handfuls of flour on the sifting basket.

triangular in shape. Both baskets are worked the same way, but Grandmother used the latter, and Julia prefers it to this day. Striving to master Grandmother's technique, Julia copied her motions, eventually becoming proficient.

To learn, Julia started practicing with one handful of flour at a time, slowly working her way up by small handfuls to the three she usually uses. She recommends this gradual learning process for others as well, with the ultimate number of handfuls being dependent on the size of an individual's hand and the size of the basket. If too much flour is placed in the basket it will "float" all over its surface, resulting in less effective sifting.

The pounded meal is spread across the basket's inner face, excepting the areas used for handholds. This insures good contact between the meal and the weave of the basket which, as will be seen, is necessary for successful sifting.

Once the flour is in the basket, Julia pushes her long sleeves out of the way, then stabilizes the basket with her hands. Proper hand and arm positioning in relation to the basket is the first step to effective sifting.

Here, Julia is still holding the wider side of the basket in her left hand after spreading acorn across it. Realizing that it doesn't feel right, she will soon turn it around so her right hand holds the wider side, her usual sifting method.

Sifting occurs as the basket vibrates between the middle and ring fingers, and the thumb of the right hand.

Coarse particles bounce off the sifting basket's lower edge and into the cooking basket. Note the finer flour clinging to the basket's weave.

This hand positioning is second nature and instantaneous to Julia, and its complexities can easily go unnoticed.

Julia holds the basket in front of herself. With her right arm extended and left arm bent at the elbow, she grasps the basket more firmly with her left hand than the right. Her right hand holds the wide end of the basket, middle and ring fingers below, thumb above; her left hand holds the narrow end. The narrow end is held above its point; the wider end held in the middle.

The fingers of the right hand are positioned so that the middle and ring fingers are curved around and below the basket's edge. The thumb is placed above the upper (concave) side of the basket just inside its edge. The pinky and index finger are extended beyond the basket's edge.

Sifting occurs as the basket is caused to vibrate vigorously up and down between the middle and ring fingers, and thumb of the right hand. The right wrist is extended and held steady but ever so slightly bent, while the right hand and lower arm are rolled sideways a short distance back and forth. Throughout, the right thumb is kept about an inch from the middle and index fingers; the left hand stays relaxed and

The basket is tapped to loosen the sifted flour. Note that the basket has once more been turned around so the hand which supports it grasps the stronger, wider area.

In lieu of a basket, the finished flour is brushed into a plastic bag.

virtually motionless, serving to support the basket.

As the thumb of the right hand contacts the inside (concave side) of the basket, a distinct thumping results. When Julia was first teaching herself to sift, she tried to imitate the pleasant thump-thump-thumping sound she remembered Grandmother making, and when she heard the right sound she knew that she had mastered the skill.

As sifting commences, the sifting basket is shaken as described while held horizontally, parallel to the ground surface. In response to the basket's motion, the heaviest, coarsest particles of pounded acorn bounce up and down on its surface. After about 10 quick shakings, the finest acorn sticks to the basket.

Then, without any interruption in the shaking, the basket is tilted gradually toward a cooking basket below. Julia finds it easier to sift into this cooking basket, rather than directly into the mortar hole, as Lucy once did. She places it at the ready either in front of herself or, rarely, at her right side.

As the basket is tilted, the coarse particles bounce off the sifting basket's lower edge or corner and into the cooking basket. Only when this happens does Julia slow the speed of her shaking a little.

When first learning to sift, Julia tried to tilt the sifting basket away from her body, which caused the coarse meal to roll off the basket's upper edge. Later, from a movie, she learned this was a Kashia Pomo method.

Julia's skill is such that she needs only one sifting to eliminate the coarse particles in the basket. Inexperienced sifters, however, may need two or three more siftings of the acorn left in the basket to insure that the flour is fine enough. Before proceeding with the second sifting, the basket is given a gentle tap-tap-tapping from below or above to loosen the remaining meal, which adheres to the basket's fine weave. The basket is tapped from below with the fingertips, or from above by curving the fingers and rapping with the back of the fingers' ends. With the circular sifter, a small, round stick with a knot on one end is used instead of fingers to tap the fine flour loose. The same basket shaking is resumed, then comes the tapping, followed by more shaking, more tapping, and so on until the desired acorn "dust" clings to the basket. It clings so well, in fact, that it's possible to turn the basket upside down without any flour coming loose.

The finished flour is swept with a soaproot brush into a separate basket for later leaching and cooking, while the coarser flour is re-pounded with

Coarse particles left over after sifting are either repounded with whole nuts or saved for later use as starter.

whole kernels or saved for next time's starter. Re-pounded flour is easier to sift than newly pounded acorn, the latter being so light and fluffy it doesn't stick to the weave as easily.

It takes at least three handfuls of sifted flour to cook a basket of acorn. Three handfuls of crushed acorn result in about 1¼ handfuls of sifted flour.

Finally, when sifting is complete, any coarse particles remaining in and around the mortar hole are re-pounded with handfuls of whole nuts and sifted anew, or saved for next time's starter. The mortar and sifting basket are swept clean with the curved fibers of a soaproot brush. Cleanliness was and is always uppermost.

> *Lucy was immaculate. Boy, her baskets were scrubbed clean.*
> *And rocks. Her special rocks. She just kept everything just so.*
> *Not sloppy. Her rock. Scrub her old rock off. Keep it clean.*
> *Very, very immaculate.*

*Leaching acorn in Yosemite Valley, 1913. Suzie Georgely (Chukchansi Yokuts)
is standing on the left. Photo by Ora Baring, YNPRL-3778.*

Leaching

Acorn contains bitter-tasting tannic acid. After the flour is sifted, this tannic acid is washed (leached) away in a sand basin. Comparable to pouring hot water over coffee grounds for a morning's drink, leaching involves pouring cold water through the sifted flour. However, unlike manzanita cider and coffee, it's the flour, not the water, which is saved.

For leaching, the basin is first formed in a mound of sand. The sand is loosened with a shovel, abalone shell, hand, stick, or piece of wood, then moved and patted into a form resembling a flattened volcano or tall saucer.

Precision in loosening the sand is essential, lest the water drain through too slowly. Alice Wilson was especially concerned about this, telling Julia the acorn would get mad if the basin wasn't properly porous and fluffy.

Weather can contribute to slow leaching. Rain makes the basin and the ground beneath it soggy and especially slow to drain. Snow or cold temperatures can cause moisture in the basin to freeze. To keep her basin dry and prevent cats and other animals from digging around in it, Lucy covered it with a canvas tarp. If it's frozen or wet from rain, for her part, Julia shovels the sand.

> See what I do is I get way down in there, and I just upset the whole thing. See 'cause with all the moisture and the rain, the sand packs see. And then if you get up and shake it up and loosen it up, it will go through. You need to do a big area. If you want your acorn to leach fast, you do a big area.

95

Precision in loosening the sand is essential, lest the water drain through too slowly.

Once the sand is loose, Julia forms it into a saucer with her hands, skillfully shaping the lipped sides and lightly compacting the sand as she goes. So the leaching water will spread evenly across the basin, like the ladies Julia uses water in a pie tin as a leveler. The sand is levelled by running the tin across the bottom of the basin. At times, like Lucy, Julia takes a square piece of board or shingle, twisting and scraping its edge against the sand until the bottom of the basin is even and level. A basket or cup with water also works. Anything that's flat.

Julia uses water in a pie tin to level the sand.

The basin is several inches deep and sometimes a yard or more across. Its width and depth depend on the amount of acorn to be leached and the type of ground the basin is built atop.

In olden times acorn was taken to the sandy edges of a river for leaching. Nowadays, sand is brought to the area where the acorn will be leached. (Lucy Telles hauled sand from the banks of the Merced River to her yard.) If the soil beneath the sand is clayey, the leaching water won't be absorbed into the ground, so the basin must be deep enough to absorb the full amount of water needed to leach a given amount of acorn.

Once completed, the basin should accommodate a layer of flour less than one-half inch deep, ideally one-eighth to one-quarter inch. If the

Sometimes, a board is also used for leveling.

flour is any deeper, it will take too long to leach — the thinner the layer, the faster it will leach, and if it is too deep, the water will hardly go through at all. A bed about 24 inches across and 10 or more inches deep with about a 2-inch lip will accomodate 4 handfuls of sifted flour. The higher the sand pile, the quicker the water will go through.

In the olden times, pine needles were sometimes used to line the basin. Sometimes the acorn flour was laid directly atop the sand (see appendix). Since the late 1800s, however, it has been customary to cover the basin with a cloth.

While Lucy's basin was always cloth-covered sand, which is what Julia uses, her neighbor Chris Brown had another way to make his basin. He'd put the sand over a pile of pine needles, then lay the cloth atop that.

Whatever the construction method, the utmost care was taken to make sure no sand entered the food. When no lining was used, the acorn was allowed to dry and harden before it was removed from the basin. After this, any acorn to which sand adhered was placed in a cooking basket partially filled with water and, after the sand had settled to the bottom, the acorn was decanted off.

Julia uses medium-weight muslin or flour or rice sacks to cover her basins. A thin cloth is selected so the leaching water will drain quickly.

While the leaching basin (in lower left corner of photo) was being made, the cooking tools, basket and leaching cloth were soaked in a bucket of water. Julia keeps a towel tucked into her skirt to clean her hands.

Before being placed on the basin, the cloth is soaked in a pail of water, then excess water is wrung out.

The selected cloth is laid atop the basin slowly so that no dirt, sand, or dust gets on it. Lucy, who only leached in early mornings, needed nothing to hold the edges of the cloth down. However, in Julia's sunny, often breezy demonstration area, the edges of the cloth dry quickly, so they are often secured with small rocks.

The Paiute ladies on the East Side of the Sierra built brush fences to protect the leaching basin from being blown by desert winds. Julia recalls these windbreaks as being made by intertwining sagebrush and willow between upright poles, but is unsure of their construction details. At one point she thought of making her own windbreak but, since she never saw Lucy using one, decided against it.

Once the basin is ready, Julia uses her hand to mix the sifted acorn flour with cold water in a galvanized metal bucket. Although some people use warm water, Julia prefers the cold for convenience and tradition. After being thoroughly mixed, the acorn/water mixture is poured into the leaching basin, where the coarser particles of acorn will sink to the bottom of the basin, while the fine particles — the "fines" — will float within any water which has not yet drained through the sand. As the water drains, these fine particles settle upon the coarse. The fines are cooked into soup (*akiva*), a wonderful, hot drink the consistency of tomato or mushroom soup, or a thick malt. The rest is cooked into mush (*nuppa*) or "water biscuit" (*uhlley*), also called "acorn roll," "acorn buns" or "jelly roll."

While the acorn/water mixture is poured into the basin, Julia keeps it moving by swishing the water in the bucket with her hands and gently swirling the bucket. This is critical if the acorn is to form two layers in the leaching basin. If the acorn is not kept suspended in the water, the coarsest acorn will settle to the bottom of the bucket and only the fines will end up in the basin.

Once drained, a smooth, even, yellow blanket of moist acorn sits atop the basin. Julia presses out any lumps she discovers with a fingertip. This attention to detail is necessary because flour in lumps might not get completely leached, which would affect the taste of the food.

The acorn is allowed to drain for up to about 20 minutes, until it becomes packed down and is nearly dry, but not so dry it will crack. This causes the acorn to stick together, insuring not a grain of acorn will be disturbed as more leaching water is poured.

After the leaching cloth is removed, the cooking tools and basket are left soaking in the bucket.

The ease with which the first pouring drains is the true measure of a well built leaching bed. If the water drains sluggishly, it isn't possible to remove the cloth and its acorn, move the sand around, and improve the drainage. For some reason, the wet acorn will never properly separate into layers if remixed with water and re-poured onto the cloth; instead, fine and coarse will remain together, impeding leaching.

> . . . once you get it into that sand, you have to continue to leach it. If it takes all night, you've got to let it drain . . . But once it gets mixed with water and it drains down and it's on that cloth and you take it off and you try to mix it with water, it won't mix.

In preparation for further leaching, a waterbreak is made to absorb the force of leaching water as it is poured atop the acorn, preventing holes from forming in the meal, and thereby insuring even leaching. A small bundle of incense cedar or white fir boughs is selected for this purpose. Although Lucy used incense cedar exclusively, Julia uses white fir as well, finding its appearance pleasing.

Bound with a cloth strip, string or branchlet at the end opposite the bough's tips, the waterbreak is rinsed clean of any dust and then placed across one side of the basin. The bound end is balanced against the basin's edge. The boughs sit atop the meal, a lovely green contrasting with the pale yellow of the acorn.

Clear water from the now refilled bucket is poured slowly from silver tin cups, white porcelain bowls, or enamel pots onto the waterbreak until a thin, clear layer of water spreads over the entire mass, completely filling the basin. The layer, like a miniature reflecting pool, must completely cover the meal lest it leach unevenly.

While the pool of water is present, additional cupfuls of water are poured along the inside, lipped edges of the basin; or fingertips are used to splash some water from the pool onto the lipped edges. This washes down any acorn flour which splashed up above the rest during the initial bucket pouring.

> If you don't get all of that acorn powder wet, and you leach the rest of it that's in the bed, it's going to have that bitter taste in it. It'll make your . . . acorn mush bitter then. So it's real important to get all that little flour down in with the rest of the flour as you leach it. The only way that you can remedy that is if you cover that, all of the acorn with water, you know. So you

Once the basin is ready, Julia uses her hand to mix the sifted acorn flour with cold water.

> have to fill that basin all the way up. But this way you can
> eliminate that by just making sure that it washes back down
> into the acorn itself.

The pool is ephemeral, growing smaller and smaller as it quickly drains into the sand. Unlike the initial pouring of the acorn/water mixture, from here on out, the leaching water is not usually allowed to completely drain. Instead, more water is continually poured directly onto the water-break or, when there is a lot of water in the basin, against the inside lipped edges of the basin. Either way, care is taken not to disturb the meal. From time to time, bits of leaves or sticks which may fall onto the water are removed with fingertips.

About half an hour and ten or eleven buckets of water later, the initial eight to ten cups of acorn are "sweet," without any trace of bitterness, and transformed from a yellow to a light beige hue. The extent of color change depends on the mineral content of the water. Where the water is especially free of impurities there is little change; where there are impurities, such as iron in the pipes, the flour turns a dark salmon color.

The proof of leaching is in the tasting. Julia lifts some flour from the

The acorn/water mixture is poured into the leaching basin.

A white fir waterbreak is placed atop the acorn on one edge of the leaching basin.

middle of the basin and samples it from her fingertip. If any bitterness is detected, leaching proceeds anew.

Once leached, the flour is left to drain for several minutes so it will be firm, not flip-floppy, when pulled away from the cloth. A thin layer of acorn, like the skin on whole milk, sits on top of the flour once thoroughly drained. This skin catches any dust or dirt which may have settled on the acorn during leaching, and is carefully scraped away with fingertips, then returned to the earth as an offering with a respectful, silent thank you.

Julia removes the leached acorn from the cloth as one unit — the "new way" — or, as learned from Lucy, in two layers. When she removes the flour as a unit, Julia first pulls the acorn away from the cloth in clumps with her fingertips. Then she places the edge of her palm against the wet flour, rolling the flour in a circle, gradually forming it into an elongated "log" which will be cooked into mush (*nuppa*). When she removes it as two layers, she first carefully sweeps the fines away from the coarser flour with her fingertips and sets them to one side of the basin to be later cooked into *akiva*. The coarse flour is then pulled away and rolled off the basin as with one layer and placed on the other side, later to be cooked into *nuppa* or water biscuit. The fines are distinguished from the coarse by appearance.

> *And you can feel it. But mostly it's by looking, you know. As soon as you pull the acorn, that top layer off, and then you go in and you just very carefully skim off the real fine one; and then if you look real carefully you can see the coarse on the bottom. And then when you're sifting it, it looks like that you've really sifted that acorn good by the feel, but when you look on that acorn you can tell that you didn't. It tells on you. That's why I say, "It tells on you."*
>
> *But it's real interesting if you look at those things. I guess I notice it more, is because when we're doing it out there all the time, I see all these things, you know. And as a rule, when you're doing it, you're not . . . aware; you're not conscious of those things happening like that to the acorn.*

Following leaching, the cloth is rinsed clean of sand, hung to dry, then cleaned as needed in a washing machine. The tannic acid sometimes leaves a light purple, inky-colored stain.

Sometimes Julia puts the leached flour directly into the cooking basket from the basin. Other times, she carries it to the cooking area in a basket lined with incense cedar fronds. The cedar adds to the flavor and keeps the basket clean, and as Julia points out, it also looks pretty.

An enamel potful of water is slowly poured onto the waterbreak.

Cooking acorn in Yosemite Valley, 1913. Photo by Ora Baring, YNPRL-13,781.

Cooking

As Grandmother before her, Julia cooks in a basket, an incredible, astounding, wondrous feat. The tan cooking baskets, which are decorated with geometrical designs of black or sienna, have a close, watertight weave. They can take several hundred hours to make.

A small sized cooking basket which is a foot wide and six inches deep will hold four handfuls of pounded and leached acorn, enough water for boiling the acorn, and up to two heated cooking stones. Lucy, who "really pounded the acorn," cooked in a huge basket thirteen inches high.

Before cooking, the basket is soaked at least two hours, enhancing its water-holding capability and preventing burning. Then the basket is placed in a shallow depression previously prepared to hold it stable during cooking. Like Lucy, Julia covers the depression with canvas, a gunnysack, an old dishcloth, or a flour sack before setting the basket down; or, in a method she innovated when these weren't available, Julia uses thimbleberry leaves to line the hole.

> *I get four great, big ones, and I lay it in there. And gee that looks so pretty with the basket sitting right in there and the leaves. And then when you have your acorn* uhlley *in the basket, and you got that spray of green in there, and the water and the* uhlley *in there. Oh, how pretty!*

When a new basket is used, a small amount of the moist, leached meal is rubbed along the inside of the lower part of its weave up to what will become the water line, further sealing the basket. Then the rest of the leached acorn to be cooked is added.

Lucy always added warm water to the cooking basket. Heated on her outside fire grill, warm water helped cook the acorn faster, along with serving as a thickening test. If the acorn will be thick, the addition of warm water will cause some thickening before cooking.

Julia, who usually doesn't have access to warm water, uses cold. The water is mixed in a ratio of about 1 cup of leached acorn to about 2½ cups of water. The volume of water varies according to the age of the acorns. Acorns stored for ten years don't thicken as readily as younger acorns, so less water is used. Less water is also used with "green" acorn, which thickens readily.

Heated stones, soapstone (steatite) or volcanic basalt, rounded and fist-sized, are used for boiling acorn. These are chosen for their ability to absorb heat readily without breaking or exploding when exposed to temperature extremes. Prior to their first use, the stones are "cured," tested in a fire to insure they won't explode unexpectedly during cooking.

Grandmother Lucy obtained river-rounded basaltic cooking stones from the rock-strewn streambed near Mirror Lake in Yosemite Valley. Julia still marvels at how "the old folks" knew just which stones to look for among the many in the riverbed.

Lucy obtained soapstone, which is relatively soft and chalky, in the Mariposa area. This was her preferred cooking stone since it absorbs heat faster than basalt. Grandmother found rounded soapstone, but Phoebe Hogan, who also preferred soapstone, found hers in chunks. Then she sawed them into a rough shape and rounded them to the desired size with a hard stone.

> When I used to cook acorn for Phoebe, she'd have her
> soapstone. She'd be out there sawing the soapstone . . .

Cooking stones are preheated in a fire. It takes 30 minutes or more for the stones to glow red and become hot enough for cooking. The length of time the rocks remain in the fire is dependent upon the type of wood which fuels it. Manzanita and oak wood make the hottest fires.

Once hot enough, the stones are removed from the fire with incense cedar or oak poles, usually by an assistant.

> I've done it by myself too. But it's always nice to have somebody
> to help you. Or what you do. You don't really ask anybody.
> That person just comes up and says, "I'll do that for you."

Cooking stones are preheated in a fire which was started just before leaching began.

Lucy was assisted by her husband, sons, grandsons, Julia, or somebody else.

Over five feet long, the poles look like giant chopsticks. Their tips, which are tapered at one end and fire-hardened, are soaked in water about an hour and a half prior to use. Such soaking prevents the poles from burning on contact with the stones. Their length insures the user's hands don't get too close to the fire. And, as Julia learned in the Indian Village all those years ago, the user's arms should be moistened periodically to keep from being singed.

One by one, the stones are lifted from the fire then dipped in quick succession into two buckets of water. Soon, paper-thin pieces of charcoal soot and black ash coat the surface of the once clear, icy cold, and clean water in the buckets, more in the first than the second.

As the rocks are lowered into the buckets, they cause the water to hiss, sizzle, and warm up. Although the stones lose some of their heat this way, the extra rinsing is insurance that the ashy buildup is thoroughly removed. The stones remain extremely hot.

Should a stone drop from the poles during rinsing, important heat is lost, so technique is important. Once a stone is wedged between the poles, an inward pressure is exerted by the left hand, which wraps around

A cooking stone receives its second rinsing in a second bucket of water. When heated red hot, very little ash is there to rinse off.

A looped stirrer is used to roll the cooking stones gently in the basket of acorn.

the poles down low. Julia uses her stronger right hand to stabilize the poles from above.

After being rinsed by an assistant, the stones are placed onto a looped stirring stick that Julia holds inside the basket just above water level while she kneels next to the basket on an old quilt, like Lucy, or a small burlap sack, or a small tule mat she has specially woven. If no assistant is available, Julia lowers the stones into the basket directly from the poles.

Looped stirrers were used by both the Southern Sierra Miwok and the Mono Lake Paiute. They are made from a carefully selected, long, straight branch of a pinyon pine (as in the case of Lucy), oak, or dogwood, which has been stripped of its bark, then bent back on itself while being heated over a fire. The handle is bound figure-eight style near the top and bottom with cloth, rag, string or a hide strip.

When it has been lowered onto the looped stirrer, the first stone is held suspended at water level in the mush as a kind of preheating agent before being lowered into the basket. As the first stone cools, another one is added. Depending on the basket's size, two or more stones may be kept in the basket at a time. Once a rock has lost considerable heat, it is removed from the basket and set on the ground next to or atop any others that have been removed, making a neat pile. First, however, any excess acorn is brushed into the basket with the hand. Since the rock is still quite hot, the hand is first dipped into a container with clean, cold water.

Once in the basket, the cooking stones are gently rolled (never pushed) to distribute their heat through the food evenly and protect the food and basket from being burned. The gentle rolling also prolongs the life of the basket by preventing the wear and tear to which it would be subjected if the stones were moved too vigorously. With prolonged use, the bases of cooking baskets do wear out. The Yosemite Miwok/Paiute repaired the base by stitching it tight with basketry material. As needed, they removed the old bases and replaced them with another or wove a new one onto the basket.

Within minutes, the mush begins to bubble, boil, blurp, and steam, filling the air with a nutty scent. Finally, four to six or more rocks later, the meal is completely cooked to the desired soup or mush consistency. Depending on the number of rocks, it may be referred to as "four-rock soup" or "six-rock soup."

The sight of acorn boiling in the basket is stunning. Julia still remembers the "oogled-eyed" astonishment she felt upon seeing her first basket of

The sight of acorn boiling in the basket is stunning.

acorn being cooked: "I'd stand there and just look at it."

While boiling, scalding hot acorn can sometimes pop out of the basket, which has necessitated a rule designed to keep the cook's attention on her work, thereby protecting the food and basket.

> *You can't be scared of it. When the hot acorn lands on you, you can't say ow. . . . You can't jump back either. You know, when it starts to pop out, you can't jump back if you get scared. That's why I don't let too many girls cook. I don't want them to get burned. . . . It will pop right up on you over your head and everything. That's why I like wearing the leather skirts out here, because if it landed on your skirt, the leather was so thick it wouldn't get burned . . .*
>
> *That's why the kids aren't supposed to be around. They could get burnt. That stuff when it comes to a full boil, especially if you've got a big basket, it's just like cornmeal mush in a pot. You put that heat to it.*

Julia further recalls of Grandmother:

> *I know she never allowed the kids to be around us when we were boiling in the basket. She said, "The kids, get away. Stay over there." It's only protecting them.*

After it has lost much of its heat, a cooking stone is removed from the cooking basket (mush boiler). It will be replaced by a hot stone from the fire. No more than three rocks at a time are kept in the mush boiler — if there are too many, they tend to stick to the basket.

When it is fully cooked, acorn has a subtle, delicate, nutty flavor. It is rarely seasoned, except by the use of one last cooking stone, which is removed from the fire, rinsed, then lowered to the surface of the acorn and moved over the top of the food to "scorch" it.

Julia learned this technique from Lucy. She also learned a Paiute seasoning method from her husband's aunt, who took clean incense cedar leaf and pounded it with acorn in the mortar.

In addition to Lucy's cooking methods, Julia is familiar with two other variations. Photographs show Maggie Howard making acorn cakes by heating a flat slab of stone with a fire, cleaning it, then laying leached acorn meal, which she had formed into small, round patties, atop the stone to cook. And Julia has observed that some Western Mono women cook the flour as a unit — rather than separating it into layers — then let it cool and congeal in the basket overnight before serving.

As learned from Lucy, Julia makes *akiva* (soup), *nuppa* (mush) or *uhlley* (water biscuit), and acorn "chips," a special treat for the children.

Chips are pieces of hardened, cooled acorn peeled off the cooking stones, which only form if the cooking stones are covered with a thick layer of acorn when they are removed from the cooking basket. Such stones are usually placed atop one another in a pile on the ground, on a clean piece of tin, or on a clean piece of bedrock. If there's only a thin layer when the stone cools, the acorn will singe and blacken as the stone sits cooling.

While Julia uses both the thin and thick layer of leached acorn as a unit to cook *nuppa*, Lucy made hers with only the thick layer, using the fines to make *akiva*.

While the ladies "just knew" when their acorn was cooked, Julia has a special test.

> In order to test it to see if it's done, I just take the acorn spoon
> and drop it in the cold water. And when it jells really quickly,
> then it's done. It's cooked. It's just like when you drop fudge
> into cold water, you know, and it jells up.

Grandmother always cooked her *nuppa* first, then used this for *uhlley*. Only occasionally, when the *nuppa* wasn't thick enough, was it eaten as is.

> See when it's old acorn, it won't ever get thick. It tends to get
> thin, you know. No matter how much acorn you put in, it
> always has that problem of getting thick.
> Because that's what happened to me last summer out there
> when I was cooking acorn. I couldn't get it thick. I think it was
> because it was old acorn. Also, too, maybe I put too much
> water in.

To make *uhlley*, Grandmother wet a small, blue-edged white porcelain bowl about 5½ inches wide and 2 inches deep with water, then dipped it into hot *nuppa*. The water acted like a lubricant, allowing the *nuppa*, which was then poured into a galvanized tub full of ice cold water and clean incense cedar fronds, to slide away from the bowl without sticking.

After a cup or so of acorn was poured into the cold water, the now tilted bowl was rolled down and then quickly jerked upright to cut off the flow of hot acorn into the tub. The rolling and jerking motion caused a pretty shell-like shape, somewhat curved in on itself, to form in the tub.

This *uhlley* jelled almost immediately upon contact with the cold water, but as more and more *uhlley* were added, the water would warm. Lucy kept hose water dribbling into the tub so that warmed water was continually replaced with cold. When it was time to eat, the *uhlley* had a refreshing foresty taste, a taste it gained as it was lifted by hand from the tub through a film of oils left by the incense cedar fronds.

Julia, who makes her *uhlley* in a cooking basket rather than a tub, pours off the water whenever it warms, replacing it with cold. After the *uhlley* has jelled, she covers it with incense cedar fronds for flavor and to keep the dust off.

Experience has shown Julia that the thickness of *nuppa* determines the quality of *uhlley*. If *nuppa* is thick, *uhlley* will be properly firm — if the *nuppa* is not thick enough, the *uhlley* will crumble when handled. Julia insures her *nuppa* will be of the proper consistency by processing "old acorn," which has been stored for three or more years, together with "new acorn," which has been stored only one or two years.

After making *uhlley*, Grandmother cooked her *akiva* in the same basket as the *nuppa*. Since *akiva* is soupier than *nuppa*, the extra water would cleanse the basket's weave of any thicker mush which adhered.

As learned from Lucy, after cooking and prior to eating Julia makes an offering of a small amount of the cooked acorn into the fire. The basket is cleaned right away by scrubbing water against the weave with a pitch-handled soaproot brush; prompt cleaning prevents the acorn from hardening in the basket, which would make cleaning difficult. The cooking stones are cleaned by peeling off any adhering food.

As Julia recalls, the "old timers" ate acorn as virtually its own meal, since they could eat everything else, like stew, tortillas, and hot sauce, any other day. To eat, they ladled the *akiva* into cups and pulled the *uhlley* out of the basket by hand.

Sometimes there was no acorn left at the end of the meal, but if any *akiva* and *uhlley* remained, Lucy usually transferred them into the same blue enamel pot for later reheating, then cleaned the basket and put it away. Keeping the *uhlley* in the *akiva* kept it from getting crusty. Occasionally, when Lucy cooked *akiva* in the morning, she saved it in the basket until later in the day, then reheated it with a couple of hot stones.

From time to time, other native foods were also eaten at the Indian Village. These included fresh wild onion tops, which were gathered in the spring and wrapped in warm tortillas, fresh watercress, also gathered in the spring, manzanita cider, pinyon pinenut soup, deer meat, fish, sourberry juice, and *koochabe*. Pinenut soup — the consistency of cream of tomato soup or a thin corn meal mush — was made by adding cold water to roasted, then pounded pinenuts. Sometimes the ladies added white wheat flour to make it stretch.

Before eating, a small amount of cooked acorn is offered into the fire.

Sourberry juice, similar to lemonade, is made much the same way as manzanita cider, by crushing sourberries in a mortar, then soaking the crushed berries in a gallon jar of water. *Koochabe*, the pupae of a shorefly (*Hydropyrus hians*)[1] which Lucy both gathered from Mono Lake and traded for, was eaten like dried shrimp.

Lumpy Acorn

One evening, thinking I had pretty well learned how to cook mush, Julia said, "And you know you can make lumpy acorn too. Do you know that?" "What?" I wondered.

> *You can make lumpy acorn. Like when you make gravy, you have lumpy gravy.*

Lumpy acorn results from adding a hot cooking stone to a cold acorn mixture. Such a situation usually results from not cooking acorn the same day it's leached, but instead storing the leached acorn in a refrigerator or freezer. If the acorn isn't warmed to room temperature, or if it isn't warmed by adding hot rather than cold water to the cooking basket, the difference in temperature between the acorn and cooking stones will result in lumps.

Another variation results from adding water after the acorn has been partially cooked. This happens during cooking, when it's realized that the acorn is too thick from adding too little water at the start.

> *That's another thing, too. When you cook acorn, the only time you put water in it is when you're getting ready to cook it, okay? If it's too thick, and you need to add water to it you can, but it's got to be hot water. . . .*
>
> *But then what's going to happen to the acorn is that when the acorn cools off, all that water that you've added after it's been partially cooked is going to come to the top of the acorn, and you'll have just a layer of water on top. But it'll be soft, so you got to mix it up again. . . . Then the water goes back into it.*
>
> *That's another trick, too. I forgot about that. We've got a lot of little things.*

The amount of water added to the basket prior to cooking is determined by sight, not measurement. I realized that I had not heard of lumpy or watery acorn because when skilled acorn cooks like Julia are done, their acorn is smooth, not lumpy.

Julia smiles in approval after tasting the nuppa.

Chris Brown (Chief Lemee), 1950, was well known for his presentations of Southern Miwok dances in the Indian Garden behind the Yosemite Museum. Photo by Ralph H. Anderson, YNPRL-14267.

Old Ways
And New

Julia's acorn making methods are true to those of Grandmother Lucy, right down to the post-contact use of galvanized buckets and cloth. When processing acorn, Julia prefers to do it this way, explaining, "We should keep the old way here because of our children, and our children's children, and generations to come after us."

Julia wants to keep alive the technology "those women . . . years ago found out about."

> *This is what fascinates me so much in anything, anything that*
> *I do, whether it's the baskets or the food . . . the high technology*
> *that they had. Also, that's what really keeps me going when*
> *you think about it.*

For Julia, the old way is also the way which produces the desired taste and cooks the acorn fastest. Julia can always tell when friends mix other acorn flour with the black oak flour she has given them. There is also a distinct difference in taste between basket- and pot-boiled acorn. The pot-boiled lacks that "nice scorched rock taste."

Acorn is precious food, and whether modern methods are used or not, Julia is committed to its continuance as a food the way it was given to the people; she has heard of non-Indians mixing acorn with wheat flour, but to her this should never be done. Not only is it not traditional, but to do this is like saying the food isn't good enough as it is. It is to make it something that isn't Indian.

Although Julia prefers the old processing methods, she hastens to say

123

that modern methods have a place, especially when the necessary baskets and other implements are unavailable: "It's all in the way you want to do things."

Some modern compromises have come about for convenience. When Julia sees acorn on the ground, she sometimes gathers it into an apron or skirt, rather than return home for her baskets. Since she demonstrates acorn making all over, unlike the past when the worksite didn't change, Julia must often haul her pestles along. She also sometimes hauls her cooking stones in a metal bucket.

While Grandmother always pounded her acorn, Alice Wilson introduced Julia to a large sized, hand-crank meat grinder. To get the acorn fine enough required running the meal through the grinder repeatedly. Since black oak is so oily, the machine became plugged from these repeated grindings, and had to be scraped out.

Another modern method involves the use of an electric blender. Phoebe Hogan was given a blender by a relative, so she and Julia tried it out. They added so much acorn at once that it got oily and the motor burned up. Julia speculates that if they had added whole acorns from time to time to absorb the oils, the flour would have remained fluffy, preventing destruction of the motor.

From Julia's perspective, a drawback of both hand-crank and electric grinders is that only one uniformly textured flour results, rather than the two textures that result from pounding and sifting. Since Julia has the requisite sifting basket and pounding rock, she has no need of a blender. She has also found she's able to pound more flour in a mortar than she could process in an electric blender in a given amount of time.

> Lucy [Julia's daughter, who is named after Lucy Telles] and I.
> That little basket I had there. Her and I used to whip that out
> in about five minutes, ten minutes pounding. She'd pound, and
> I'd pound. And I'd sift, and then she'd pound. And then I'd
> sift and pound. And we used to just get lots of flour. It's amaz-
> ing how fast.

For convenience Julia sometimes saves whole, shelled acorn — both winnowed and not — in plastic bags in the refrigerator, also placing her usual cloth bag of starter in a plastic one. The plastic keeps the acorn from absorbing refrigerator smells. She also stores leached acorn in the freezer, but never cooked. When the latter is thawed, the water and acorn separate, giving the acorn the appearance of milk curd.

If acorn is stored in the refrigerator or, in the case of leached, in the freezer, it's important to bring it to room temperature before use. Since Julia makes her acorn often and doesn't have time to thaw it, she avoids putting leached acorn in the freezer.

At times, Julia opts for relatively modern, "real fast, Betty Crocker" leaching methods. Acorn flour which has been mixed with water is poured into a cloth- or muslin-lined, flat parching basket. This is perched in her kitchen sink, and leaching undertaken as if it was a sand basin.

A more time-consuming method is available for those who lack the parching basket. It involves placing dry acorn meal in a flour or salt sack. The sacks are filled with water, which is allowed to drain, fully saturating the meal. Then the sack is tied underneath a faucet so that a very slow stream of water can drip onto it, and subsequently through the acorn all night.

After cooking, Julia stores her leftover acorn in a gallon jar in the refrigerator, where it awaits reheating in a pot on her stove. When using a pot, Julia makes sure it's stainless steel rather than aluminum, which will react (oxidize) with the acorn, turning it black.

> Because I remember over there on the East Side, the ladies were telling me too that their acorn; they put it in their pot and their acorn got black, so they didn't use that aluminum pot.

When cooking in a pot the heat is indirect — first the pot heats, then the acorn — and Julia finds the acorn tends to stick to the bottom. To prevent scorching and burning, it is important to stir it constantly for the fifteen minutes or so it takes to cook.

Once it is cooked, Julia sometimes sprinkles salt on her acorn, something that was never done in the past. Her taste for salt was acquired at Stewart Indian School, and has remained with her since that time.

*Lucy Brown (Southern Miwok) pounding whole acorn, circa 1900.
Photographer unknown, YNPRL-14,110.*

Respecting The Food

Every time Julia makes acorn she teaches respect for the food. We are reminded of how careful the elders were with food. We are reminded that you don't just sit down and make acorn. This is food. Anyone who wants to learn must take care to do things the right way. The special way.

While acorn preparation is an involved process, it is infinitely satisfying. For Julia, it provides a tangible link with preceding generations and is an enjoyable way to spend one's time. "I love it. I don't have to do it," Julia explains.

Julia makes acorn because it is a nourishing food. Not only can one feed more people with a basket of mush than with a loaf of bread, but infants can digest it. When Grandmother Lucy provided acorn to Julia's three-month-old firstborn, Julia was hesitant at first. But, like new mothers of previous generations, she learned it was fine for them. It went down like pablum.

"My grandchildren love it," Julia has found. "They would rather eat acorn mush than any other kind of cereal." She is proud that two grand-children have learned to prepare acorn by helping "grandma." Julia is also proud that the quality of her acorn is such that her husband Ralph prefers her acorn to any other and eats it exclusively.

Most importantly, Julia makes acorn because of what it represents. "I know that lots of times I think, 'Why do I do this? We don't eat it everyday. Why should I do it?' But . . . it's a special food. It was life to them in the earlier years, and it is still life to a lot of us who want to learn the ways. Who want to learn to prepare acorn to eat. . . . Then again, we should not lose the old way."

Making acorn is also a commitment to the future. "It will live forever and ever and ever, like the acorn has the tannic acid. . . . It will live on."

Appendix

Early Descriptions Of
Yosemite Acorn Making

Tourists who came to Yosemite Valley left few descriptions of Miwok/Paiute acorn preparation. Many of those descriptions that were left fall victim to stereotype.

Although sometimes incorrect, and generally lacking in details, these descriptions provide insights into the attitudes of non-Indians toward the food, as well as some preparation methods. For instance, Lafayette Bunnell, in his description of the Mariposa Battalion's activities, left us with a cursory review of Ahwahneechee acorn making in which he makes the Battalion's reaction to the food quite plain: "Although it was free from grit, and comparatively clean, none of us were able to eat it, and we were quite hungry."

Another account of Yosemite acorn preparation appeared in 1884 in a piece penned by Constance F. Gordon Cumming. Although her account is rife with value judgement, Ms. Cumming offers some interesting details on early leaching methods:

"The girls having prepared their acorn-meal in the rock cups . . . they left it to steep in cold water, to get rid of some of the bitterness, while they were building up a huge pie-dish or basin of river-sand. This they lined with fine gravel, and placed the powdered acorns in this rude dish."

She went on to describe the use of warm water for preparing acorn cakes and leaching:

"A large fire has been kindled, and a number of stones the size of your fist thrown in to bake. When they were thoroughly heated they were lifted out by a woman, holding two sticks in lieu of a pair of tongs, and were dropped into a small basket of water, which hissed and spluttered, and became black and sooty. After this preliminary washing, the hot stones were fished out and deposited in the large water basket which acted the part of kettle. Though somewhat cooled by this double process, the stones soon heated the water to a certain extent.

"A very small quantity of this tepid, singed fluid was then poured on the acorn-flour, some of which was made into paste and taken out to be baked as cakes. More water was added. A green fern-leaf was laid over the flour, apparently to enable the pouring to be done more gently — and so a large mass of porridge was prepared, and ladled out in baskets. Then — that nothing might be wasted — the gravel was taken out and washed, to save the flour still adhering to it.

"This acorn-paste becomes glutinous, and is eaten in the same way that the Pacific Islanders eat *poi*, by dipping in a finger, twirling it round, and so landing it in the mouth."

The description ends here, with no mention of cooking.

In 1893 Elizabeth Grinnell left us with the most important of the early descriptions of acorn processing, detailing methods which are no longer used. According to her observations, which were made from her camp "a hundred feet from the Merced River, with an Indian village between us and Sentinel Rock," the process was begun early in the morning. While the women prepared for the day's activities, the men gathered "wood, dried leaves and twigs, which they deposited on the river-bank, and then disappeared for the day, probably trouting down the stream."

To begin, the women opened a *chuckah*, removed "several baskets full, and carefully covered the bin." Then Grinnell states that the women shelled the acorns with their teeth. This is one of several puzzling statements in the article. When I asked Julia if she had ever heard of this, she stated she had not. Perhaps the women were cracking acorn with green, not yet fully matured shells, which are soft, or some other nut, she supposed.

Another puzzling fact is that Grinnell makes no mention of winnowing. Instead, she describes a kind of roasting process: "When the kernels were all out they were roasted on hot stones, removed one at a time with a little stick, and gathered, thus partially cooked, into baskets. This roasting took several hours, and was the most tedious part of the day's labor."

After "grinding" and sifting, the acorn was poured into "a great basket and carried down to the river. Enough water was added to make a thin batter, which was stirred with wooden paddles." Some small leaching basins were then made in the clean sand on the beach by "heaping up regular sides for strength, and smoothing out the inside. When the basins were finished, tufts of pine-needles were spread over the bottom to prevent the sand from being disturbed. Then the batter was poured in. Immediately the pine tufts rose to the surface and were skimmed off."

"The mixture then began to 'settle.' When the water had all filtered into the sand more pine needles were laid in, and more water poured on, until the process had been repeated three times. The purpose of this process was to rid the batter of the poisonous, bitter principle of the acorns, leaving only the nutritious, amber-colored flour."

The puzzling aspect of Grinnell's account continues with a description of using inordinately large-sized stones to cook with. She said that while leaching was undertaken, other women were making a fire and heating cooking stones "the size of a child's head, to a white heat."

"Then began the separating of the inferior from the superior flour. There were three grades — the coarser, which was on the surface of the reservoir; the bottom or leavings which was next to the sand filter; and between these two, the clean, fine sort.

"With the edges of the two hands, the top of the meal was scraped off into a basket, into which hot water was poured and rapidly stirred. The agitation caused the meal to separate from the sand, and it was turned off, leaving the residue of debris in the bottom. This operation, repeated three times, left a clean, coarse material for 'mush.'

"When the big basket was half-full of the acorn flour, several hot stones were thrown in. The mixture began to boil. Then dexterity, strength and skill were essential, for the stones must be constantly moved about with two strong sticks, in the hands of the alert attendant."

As stones cooled, they were "lifted out by the two sticks and replaced by a hotter one."

"At the woman's side was a basket of cold water, into which she dipped her hand while she poised a stone against the edge of the mush pot, and deftly, with two strokes, divested it of the batter. She determined the exact moment when the mush was 'done' by its adhesiveness. When it dropped from the stones of itself, leaving them bare and clean, it was properly cooked.

"The bushel basket of boiling porridge was then lifted to the back of a woman in waiting, where it was secured by a cloth which encircled its brim and passed around the forehead of the carrier. She bore it to camp, ready for succeeding breakfasts.

"It is eaten without salt or sugar, and washed down with cold water. These Indians drink neither beer nor coffee.

"Now the first layer of meal in the filtering reservoir has been disposed of, and we hasten to the next or middle portion. This was scooped out by the hooked fingers, placed in a basket, and set to one side.

"There was now nothing left in the basin but the lining coat of flour. This was peeled off with its adhering sand, and treated to several generous washings and drainings, similar to the first batch. When it was ready for the porridge pot, there was supposed to be no trace of grit in the whole basket. This was cooked by hot stones as was the first, and sent to camp as second quality.

"All this has been but incidental to the making of the real bread. That best, middle meal, which had been set to one side in a basket, was then made into a thicker batter than for mush, and was consequently harder to stir. It was cooked for a long time, and with great labor in agitating the hot stones.

"When the bread was ready to be made into loaves, the women took off a portion of their clothes and waded a little way into the river, where was an eddy, but no current. Here, with the same paddles which had stirred the mush, they scooped a hole in the bottom sand under water, and banked up the sides just high enough to allow the play of the eddy over the brim.

"Small baskets were then filled with the boiling dough and taken to the pool, where they were plunged again and again into the cold water. A little shaking from side to side, as the baskets came dripping to the surface, together with the rapid cooling, caused the bread to loosen from the baskets in free, ball-like masses.

"At the right minute the baskets were inverted, and the 'loaves' slipped out into the pool, where they could bob about without the least danger of floating down stream.

"There were a great many of these loaves, each resembling in appearance and texture a rubber ball, and they had about the same taste to my palate. They were of the size of a baker's ten-cent loaf, hard and heavy, of a light amber color. After they had remained in the river two or three hours they were perfectly cold, and ready to 'keep.'

"By this time the sun was setting and the men could be seen coming home to supper. The loaves were fished out of the water and carried to the camps in baskets, where they were deposited on the summer scaffoldings about the huts, to be drawn upon as needed, until the next baking-day should come around in about three weeks."

In 1907, one-time park guardian Galen Clark left us with a sympathetic description of *chuckah* building and acorn making. Among the early accounts, Clark's description is notable for its reference to how "elaborately prepared" acorn is and his inconclusive observation that the kernel is "pounded or ground," the first of three uses of the word "pounding" in reference to this process that appear in these accounts.

Clark describes the use of fir as a waterbreak, and leaching the acorn directly on sand with warm water heated by stones in a basket. How the leached acorn is then "cleansed from the adhering sand" is not described. Clark also describes three ways of eating the cooked acorn — as a mush, "water biscuits," and bread:

"When the dough is well cooked it is either left *en masse* in the basket or scooped out in rolls and put into cold water to cool and harden before being eaten. Sometimes the thick paste is made into cakes and baked on hot rocks. One of these cakes, when rolled in paper, will in a short time saturate it with oil. This acorn food is probably more nutritious than any of the cereals."

An article (date unknown) by Florence Brubaker of the Yosemite School of Field Natural History provides another use of the word "pounded." In it, Ms. Brubaker describes a chance encounter with Maggie "Tabuce" Howard. As Florence writes of Tabuce:

"Her son was coming over for a visit and, as a special treat, Maggie was pounding a quantity of acorns for 'biscuits.' Being questioned, she in formed [sic] us that she used 'white men's bread' until she became tired of it, then reverted to her acorn bread.

"Contrary to my preconceived ideas, she pounded, rather than ground the acorns."

In May of 1912, Harry T. Fee, in an article published in the *Overland Monthly*, commented on a blending of tradition in one woman's kitchen, where he noticed a bowl of acorn mush, fried potatoes, bacon, a shaker of salt, and a can of pepper.

In July of 1914, Frank T. Lea wrote about the continuing importance of acorn in Yosemite. He noted that at the "first of October" the women could be seen out "collecting" acorn with the traditional burden baskets, and that "great piles of acorns" were "collected" and dried in the sun, "some to be eaten at once, some to be stored in the 'chuckahs'. . . ."

Lea went on to describe acorn making as the job of older women, who made enough acorn for the entire community. He also described the use of a hammerstone for cracking acorn by a woman identified only as "Lucy:" "In front of Lucy was a flat stone, and in one hand another round one about the size of an egg, with which she cracked the nuts."

Lea wrote about "pounding" and sifting, which was completed as the day ended, then mentioned that the cooking would take place the following day. Following a description of leaching, he observed, "This washing and cooking requires plenty of water, so rather than carry water to camp they carry baskets and meal to the river, and select a nice lot of clean sand for the kitchen. A large, shallow hole is scooped out in the sand and carefully lined with leaves or a piece of cloth; on this the meal is poured and carefully covered with cold water." Concurrent to the leaching, a fire was made in which "a number of smooth stones about the size of large apples, are made hot."

Then the meal was removed from the leaching pit, "care being taken not to get any sand in it." It was placed in a basket, no pots and pans being in evidence. "Some of the baskets are woven water-tight, and some are coated with rosin [probably melted pitch and charcoal] to make them tight."

The cooking stones were removed one by one from the fire with looped stirrers, rinsed of ash in a basket of water, then placed in the cooking basket, which was rosin-coated, and partially filled with water:

"Stone after stone is thus dropped, until the water begins to boil; wet meal is added, handful at a time. All the while the pot is kept boiling by adding more hot stones as the cooling ones are taken out.

"At the proper time all the stones are taken out, the cooking is finished, and only the cooling remains, which is done in one of two ways; if the meal has been cooked very stiff it is made into round loaves [*uhlley*] and put into the river to cool, or if the cooking had not been carried quite so far, cooked meal is put into baskets to cool like blanc mange."

On April 13, 1929, the Stockton, California *Record* presented a somewhat detailed description of storing, cracking, shelling, "grinding," leaching, and cooking acorn. The article, written by Information Ranger James V. Lloyd, started by describing the importance of acorn to Miwok/Paiute people contemporary to the time of its writing: "Fifty barley sacks of acorns instead of fifty sacks of wheat, will be found in the local Indian village, where the ground acorn has never been replaced by wheat flour as the staff of life."

Lloyd went on to describe "gathering" by women who "hold the free corners of their colorful aprons in one hand and gather bushels of the full, rich nuts with their other hand until their aprons will hold no more. Then, into an empty barley sack for storage."

He describes the use of mortar holes "several inches deep" and the use of sand-leaching basins covered by a "fiber mat or cloth." In his account, hot water is used for leaching. He then states that the cooked acorn is eaten as either mush or water biscuits, describing how to make the latter as follows:

"The mush-like substance is ready for serving by dipping into the basket for a handful or it may be scooped up in smaller baskets and placed in the creek. The action of the cold water playing around the outside of the basket will cause the acorn mush to shrink, so that upon cooling it can be picked out of the basket as a rounded loaf of bread. The latter is placed on a rock to dry and harden. In a few days the bread is ready for eating. It resembles the old army 'hardtack biscuit,' as it can be carried for weeks by the Indians and still be nutritious upon eating."

Some early descriptions allude to the importance of acorn in the trade economy. On October 29th, 1869, the *Mariposa Gazette* reported that the acorns were so abundant that year that more than 50 Paiute people journeyed across the mountains for them.

The September 28, 1928, Fresno *Bee* commented on the "large number of Indian women that have reached the valley during the past week from across the mountains near Mono Lake. The gathering of the acorn crop by the Indians is a practice of long standing. Although store flour of the white man is extensively used by the Indians, they still relish the powdered acorn meal for bread."

Acorns were also mentioned as weather predictors. In an apparent media blitz by park information officers, three California newspapers, the November 1929 Fresno *Bee*, Modesto *News Herald*, and Long Beach *Sun* all announced that, according to the Indians, the year's heavy crop of acorns meant a lot of snow and ice in the coming winter. A November 1932 newspaper clipping of unknown origin stated that, "Plenty of snow and a good winter for snow sports are being predicted by members of the Yosemite Indian Village following the heaviest acorn crop since 1898."

It continued, "So thickly have the acorns covered the ground that the

Indians have discontinued gathering them after a bountiful harvest. The remainder are being stored by bears, deer and squirrels. . . .

"Pioneer members of the tribe declare 'plenty of acorns mean plenty of snow.' "

Acorn also became the subject of another piece of tourist propaganda. Under the headline, "Acorn Flour Curbs Fat, Yosemite Tourists Told," the Newark, New Jersey *Call*'s July 20, 1930 edition touted, "Young ladies desiring to avoid 'that future silhouette' should eat acorn bread. This is the advice of old Maggie [Howard]. . . ."

The article concluded, "The acorn flour demonstration is proving of great interest to hundreds of people visiting the museum, according to Park Naturalist C. A. Harwell. While Maggie does not make a practice of telling stout tourists how to grow thin, she does hint that acorn bread keeps 'that coming shadow within.' "

Bibliography

Alvarez, Susan H., and David W. Peri. Acorns: The Staff of Life *in* News from Native California. Berkeley: Heyday Books. 1(4):10-14. September/November 1987.

Anonymous. The Yosemite Valley. Another Claim Raised Against it. Mariposa, California, *Gazette*. August 20, 1869.

Anonymous. Mono Squaws Harvest Acorns in Yosemite. Fresno, California, *Bee*. September 28, 1928.

Anonymous. Squaws Wrangle With Bears Over Yosemite Acorns. Fresno,California, *Bee*. November 7, 1929.

Anonymous. Bears Eat All Acorns; Squaws Make No Bread. Long Beach, California, *Sun*. November 10, 1929.

Anonymous. Bears Gettum All Acorns, Says Ung-Wah-Tootah. Modesto, California, *News Herald*. November 17, 1929.

Anonymous. Indian Foods to Be Shown in Yosemite. Oakland, California, *Post Enquirer*. May 16, 1930.

Anonymous. Acorn Flour Curbs Fat, Yosemite Tourists Told. Newark, New Jersey, *Call*. July 20, 1930.

Anonymous. Acorns Are Many, Indians Predict Snowy Winter. November 1932.

Anonymous. Seattle Next Stop for Royal Couple. Santa Barbara, California, *News-Press*. A-5. Monday, March 7, 1983.

Anonymous. The Indian People of Ahwahnee. Yosemite Association. March 1988.

Barrett, S. A., and E. W. Gifford. Miwok Material Culture *in* Bulletin of Milwaukee Public Museum. 2(4):142-148. March 1933. (Reprinted by Yosemite Natural History Association, Inc., Yosemite National Park.)

Bates, Craig. The Reflexed Sinew-backed Bow of the Sierra Miwok *in* Ethnic Technology Notes. San Diego: San Diego Museum of Man. No. 16. December 1978.

Bates, Craig D. Names and Meanings for Yosemite Valley *in* Yosemite Nature Notes. Yosemite National Park: Yosemite Natural History Association. 47(3): 43. 1978.

Bates, Craig D. Yosemite Miwok/Paiute Basketry: A Study in Cultural Change *in* American Indian Basketry. 2(4):3-22. August 1982.

Bates, Craig D. Lucy Telles: A Supreme Weaver of the Yosemite Miwok/Paiute *in* American Indian Basketry 2(4):23-29. August 1982.

Bates, Craig D. Acorn Storehouses of the Yosemite Miwok *in* The Masterkey. Los Angeles: Southwest Museum. 57(1):19-27. January-March, 1983.

Bates, Craig D. Personal communication, 1991.

Baty, Margaret. Personal communication, August 1988.

Brubaker, Florence. When the Yosemite Indians Made Acorn. (Date and newspaper unknown.)

Bryan, Bruce. The Manufacture of Stone Mortars. Los Angeles: Southwest Museum Leaflets Number 34, pages 1-8. 1970.

Bunnell, Lafayette. Discovery of the Yosemite and The Indian War of 1851 which led to that event. Chicago: R. H. Revell, pages 40-41, 49, 66-67, 71, 72, 73, 74, 80-81, 84, 87-89, 101, 104, 108-109, 115, 1880. (Republished in 1977 by Outbooks, Olympic Valley, California.)

Clark, Galen. Indians of the Yosemite Valley and Vicinity, Their History, Customs and Traditions. Yosemite Valley, California: Galen Clark, pages 38-44. 1907. (Reprinted in 1987 by Diablo Books, Walnut Creek, California.)

Crampton, C. Gregory, editor. The Mariposa Indian War 1850-1851, Diaries of Robert Eccleston: The California Gold Rush, Yosemite, and the High Sierra. Salt Lake City: University of Utah Press. 1975.

Cumming, Constance F. Gordon. Granite Crags. Edinburgh and London: William Blackwood and Sons, pages 139-141. 1984.

Downey, Kim. Indian Interpreter Learns, Teaches Old Ways. Santa Barbara, California, *News-Press* Travel Section, E-12. Sunday, May 29, 1983.

Fee, Harry T. The Indians of Yosemite Valley *in* Overland Monthly. 59:469-471. May 1912.

Fulwider, Olive. Personal communication, 1989.

Gifford, E. W. California Balanophagy *in* Essays in Anthropology Presented to A. L. Kroeber. Berkeley and Los Angeles: University of California Press, pages 87-98. 1936. (Reprinted in 1971 *in* The California Indians, A Source Book, compiled and edited by R. F. Heizer and M. A. Whipple. Berkeley and Los Angeles: University of California Press, pages 301-305.)

Heizer, Robert, and Albert B. Elsasser. The Natural World of the California Indians. Berkeley, Los Angeles, and London: University of California Press, pages 91-100. 1981.

Godfrey, Elizabeth. Yosemite Indians. Yosemite Natural History Association: Yosemite National Park, pages 11-13, 15. 1941, 1951, 1973, 1977.

Grinnell, Elizabeth. Making Acorn Bread *in* The Youth's Companion. 66-67:559. November 2, 1893. (Reprinted in 1958 *in* Reports of the University of California Archaeological Survey, Number 41, pages 42-45, Department of Anthropology, U.C. Berkeley.)

LaPena, Frank, and Craig D. Bates. Legends of the Yosemite Miwok. Yosemite National Park: Yosemite Natural History Association, pages 9-14, 37-38, 43. 1981.

Lea, Frank T. Indian Bread Makers in Yosemite *in* Overland Monthly. 64:24-26. July 1914.

Lee, Martha J., and Craig D. Bates. The Indian Cultural Museum, A Guide to the Exhibits. Yosemite National Park: Yosemite Association, pages 1-4. 1987.

Lloyd, James V. Storing of the Acorn Crop in the Yosemite. Stockton, California, *Record*. April 29, 1929.

Mayer, Peter J. Miwok Balanophagy: Implications for the Cultural

Development of Some California Acorn-Eaters. Berkeley: Archaeological Research Facility, University of California, Department of Anthropology. 1976.

McCarthy, Helen. Bedrock Mortars: A Functional Model from the Western Mono or The Paha, Mono Style Cuisinart Plus a Basic Guide to Gourmet Acorn Processing. Fair Oaks, California: Theodoratus Cultural Research. Paper presented at the Third Annual California Indian Conference at Santa Barbara Museum of Natural History, October 16-18, 1987.

McRae, Janis. Miwok Indian Traditions Thrive Under Guidance from Julia Parker. Merced Sun-Star Living Section, A4. Monday, September 25, 1989.

Merriam, C. Hart. The Mourning Ceremony at Bald Rock Rancheria, 1907 *in* Studies of California Indians. Berkeley and Los Angeles: University of California Press, pages 61-63, 1955.

Ortiz, Bev. It Will Live Forever: Yosemite Indian Acorn Preparation *in* News from Native California. Berkeley: Heyday Books. 2(5):24-28. November/December 1988.

Ortiz, Bev. Things Have Changed *in* News from Native California. Berkeley: Heyday Books. 2(6):22-24. January/February 1989.

Ortiz, Bev. Food for Sharing *in* News from Native California. Berkeley: Heyday Books. 3(3):25-27. July/August 1989.

Parker, Julia. Written interview with Bev Ortiz. March 5, 1986.

Parker, Julia. Taped interview with Bev Ortiz. September 13 and 14, 1986.

Parker, Julia. Taped interview with Bev Ortiz. June 5, 1988.

Parker, Julia. Taped interview with Bev Ortiz. August 7, 1988.

Parker, Julia. Taped interview with Bev Ortiz. April 1, 1990.

Parker, Julia. Written interviews with Bev Ortiz. June 1-2, 1990.

Parker, Julia, and Smith, Kathleen. Taped interviews with Bev Ortiz. August 20-21, 1990.

Parker, Julia. Taped interview with Bev Ortiz. January 6, 1991.

Parker, Julia. Written interviews with Bev Ortiz. January 23-25, 1991.

Parker, Julia. Written interviews with Bev Ortiz. February 28, 1991.

Parker, Julia. Taped interviews with Bev Ortiz. March 18-19, 1991.

Parker, Julia. Written interviews with Bev Ortiz. March 18-19, 1991.

Parker, Julia. Taped interview with Bev Ortiz. May 12, 1991.

Parker, Julia. Written interviews with Bev Ortiz. May 28-29, 1991.

Parker, Julia. Taped interview with Bev Ortiz. June 9, 1991.

Parker, Julia. Written interview with Bev Ortiz. July 20 and 22, 1991.

Peri, David W. Plant of the Season: Oaks *in* News From Native California. Berkeley: Heyday Books. 1(5):6-9. November/December 1987.

Powers, Stephen. Tribes of California *in* Contributions of North American Ethnology, Volume III. Department of the Interior, U.S. Geographical and Geological Survey of the Rocky Mountain Region. Washington: Government Printing Office. 1877. (Reprinted in 1976 by University of California Press, Berkeley, Los Angeles, and London.)

Presnall, C.C. Yosemite Indians Revive Old Customs *in* Yosemite Nature Notes. X(10):84-85. October 1931.

Ross, George. Lucy Telles, Basketmaker *in* Yosemite Nature Notes. 27(4). Yosemite Natural History Association: Yosemite National Park. April 1948.

Sutton, Mark Q. Insects as Food: Aboriginal Entomophagy in the Great Basin *in* Ballena Press Anthropological Papers No. 33 (Thomas C. Blackburn, editor). Novato and Menlo Park: Ballena Press, pages 43-49. 1988.

Sward, Susan. Ghostly Tales of Queen's Yosemite Suite. *San Francisco Chronicle*, Monday, March 7, 1983.

Notes

Acorn: Food Since the Beginning

1. La Pena, Frank, and Craig D. Bates, 1981, *Legends of the Yosemite Miwok*. Yosemite National Park: Yosemite Natural History Association, pp. 13-14.

2. La Pena and Bates, 1981, pp. 13-14.

3. Powers, Stephen, 1877, "Tribes of California" in *Contributions of North American Ethnology*, Volume III. Department of the Interior, U.S. Geographical and Geological Survey of the Rocky Mountain Region. Washington: Government Printing Office (reprinted in 1976 by University of California Press, Berkeley, Los Angeles and London), pp. 363, 364, Figure 35.

The Miwok/Paiute People of Yosemite Valley

1. Bates, Craig, 1978, "Names and Meanings for Yosemite Valley" in *Yosemite Nature Notes*, 47(3). Yosemite National Park: Yosemite Natural History Association, p. 43.

2. Lee, Martha J., and Craig D. Bates, 1987, *The Indian Cultural Museum, A Guide to the Exhibits*. Yosemite National Park: Yosemite Association, p. 1.

3. Barrett, S.A., and E.W. Gifford, 1933, "Miwok Material Culture" in *Bulletin of Milwaukee Public Museum* 2(4) (reprinted by Yosemite Natural History Association, Inc., Yosemite National Park), pp. 140-178.

4. Barrett and Gifford, pp. 178-192.

5. Barrett and Gifford, p. 251; Lee and Bates, p. 2; Bates, Craig, 1978, "The Reflexed Sinew-backed Bow of the Sierra Miwok" in *Ethnic Technology Notes*, San Diego: San Diego Museum of Man, No. 16, December 1978.

6. Barrett and Gifford, pp. 257-70.

7. Bates, Craig D., 1982, "Yosemite Miwok/Paiute Basketry: A Study in Cultural Change" in *American Indian Basketry* 2(4), pp. 7-8.

8. Crampton, C. Gregory, ed., 1975, *The Mariposa Indian War 1850–1851. Diaries of Robert Eccleston: The California Gold Rush, Yosemite, and the High Sierra*. Salt Lake City: University of Utah Press, pp. i-v; and Bunnell, Lafayette, 1880, *Discovery of the Yosemite and The Indian War of 1851 which led to that event*. Chicago: R. H. Revell (republished in 1977 by Outbooks, Olympic Valley, California), pp. 12-13.

9. Bunnell, p. 27.

10. Bunnell, pp. 40-41.

11. Bunnell, pp. 48-50.

12. Today, many people refer to *Pinus sabiniana* as bull or gray leaf rather than digger pine, preferring it to the term used by non-Indians as a derogatory description of California Indians.

13. Bunnell, p. 71.

14. Bunnell, p. 73.

15. Bunnell, p. 73.

16. Crampton, p. 49.

17. Bunnell, p. 80.

18. Bunnell, pp. 104-105.

19. Bunnell, pp. 108-9, 111, 113, 115.

20. Lee and Bates, pp. 3-4.

21. Lee and Bates, pp. 4, 14.

The Telles Family

1. Bates, Craig D., 1982, "Yosemite Miwok/Paiute Basketry: A Study in Cultural Change" in *American Indian Basketry*, 2(4), p. 7; and Bates, Craig D., 1991, personal communication.

2. Bates (1982), *American Indian Basketry*, 2(4), pp. 12-13, 23-27.

Strict Attention to Detail

1. Presnall, C.C., 1931, "Yosemite Indians Revive Old Customs" in *Yosemite Nature Notes* X(10), pp. 84-85.

2. Heizer, Robert, and Albert B. Elsasser, 1981, *The Natural World of the California Indians*. Berkeley, Los Angeles and London: University of California Press, pp. 92, 95, 96, 98; and Peri, David W., 1987, "Plant of the Season: Oaks" in *News from Native California*, 1(5), Berkeley: Heyday Books, pp. 26-28.

Drying and Storing

1. Bates, Craig D., 1983, "Acorn Storehouses of the Yosemite Miwok" in *The Masterkey*, 57(1), Los Angeles: Southwest Museum, pp. 19-27.

Pounding

1. Fulwider, Olive, 1989, personal communication.

2. McCarthy, Helen, 1987, "Bedrock Mortars: A Functional Model from the Western Mono or The Paha, Mono Style Cuisinart Plus a Basic Guide to Gourmet Acorn Processing." Fair Oaks, California: Theodoratus Cultural Research. Paper presented at the Third Annual California Indian Conference at Santa Barbara Museum of Natural History, p. 5.

3. Ortiz, Bev, 1989, "Things Have Changed" in *News from Native California* 2(6). Berkeley: Heyday Books, p. 23.

4. McCarthy, p. 5.

Cooking

1. Sutton, Mark Q., 1988, "Insects as Food: Aboriginal Entomophagy in the Great Basin" in *Ballena Press Anthropological Papers* No. 33 (Thomas C. Blackburn, ed.). Novato and Menlo Park: Ballena Press, pp. 45-47.

Julia F. Parker's New Way Acorn

Cracking

Crack 4 pounds of acorn with a hammer. When cracking, tap shells
lightly enough that the nutmeats will split into halves or thirds, but
won't shatter into small pieces.

Shelling

Remove shells by hand, returning shells and any bad nuts to the earth.

Cleaning

To loosen skins, lay acorn on a cloth on a table in the sun.
Split grooves open by pressing down with the sharp edge of a knife
held lengthwise in the groove.
Sprinkle the acorns with water and allow to dry.
Rub handfuls of nutmeats between hands to remove skins.
Scrape any adhering skins off with a knife.

Taking bad nuts into account, 4 pounds result in about 4 cups of whole,
cleaned acorn.

Blender crushing

Measure out 4 cupfuls of whole, cleaned nutmeats.
Put 1 cupful (5½ oz.) in a blender and break up at low speed. The
acorn will jump all around in the blender.
Once the nutmeats are broken up, switch the blender to high speed
and run until no more acorn falls from the edges onto the blades.

Mix acorn up with the handle of a wooden spoon, making sure to include the acorn nearest the bottom, which tends to get sticky.

Repeat blending and mixing until acorn is reduced to fine flour. (If acorn gets oily as blended, add a few whole nutmeats at low speed to absorb the oils.)

Remove the now fluffy flour and set aside in a bowl.

Add second cupful and repeat process.

Add third cupful and repeat.

Add fourth cupful and repeat.

This results in 5 fluffy cupfuls of flour.

Note

If there are chunks of acorn in the flour, it needs to be run through the blender again. Don't put more than a cup of acorn in the blender at a time — any more might cause the motor to burn out.

Leaching

Put flour into a 5-pound flour, sugar or salt sack. Fill the sack full of water and allow it to drain so the flour is saturated. Tie the sack to a faucet and turn the faucet on just past a drip, so that a very slow, steady stream of water drips over the outside of the sack (which serves as a waterbreak) all night long.

Cooking

Place leached acorn (when wet, it reduces again to 4 cups) in a stainless steel pot.

Add 3 cups water and mix with acorn.

Cook at high heat, stirring frequently. While acorn cooks, gradually add 7 more cups of water.

Keep stirring.

Let the acorn boil for 15 minutes, until it has the consistency of tomato soup. For cornmeal mush consistency, add less water.

Makes 11½ cups *nuppa*.

If using fresh (newly gathered) acorn, increase the amount of water used, as fresh acorn thickens more than older acorn.